THE
CARTOON HISTORY
OF
BRITAIN

THE CARTOON HISTORY OF BRITAIN

Michael Wynn Jones

Foreword by *Cummings* of The Daily Express

TOM STACEY

ACKNOWLEDGEMENTS

The major, and quite indispensable, source for all the anonymous prints and satires from 1720 to 1800 is the British Museum Print Room, whose staff have been unfailingly helpful in my researches, and the British Museum catalogue of political and personal satires. My thanks are also due to the library staffs of the Victoria and Albert Museum and the Westminster Central Art Library, as well as all of the magazines and newspapers listed below, and Norman Hollands. The following is a very brief list, only of books on the subject which are readily available.

English Political Caricature, vols 1 and 2: M. Dorothy George (O.U.P.)
Hogarth and English Caricature: ed. F. D. Klingender
Hogarth, the Complete Engravings: Joseph Burke and Colin Caldwell (Thames and Hudson)
The Drawings of William Hogarth: A. P. Oppé (Phaidon Press)
Hogarth to Cruikshank, Social Change in Graphic Satire: M. Dorothy George (Allen Lane)
Fashionable Contrasts: Draper Hill (Phaidon Press)
Comic Art in England: C. Veth
Social Caricature in the 18th Century: George Paston

Cartoons and Caricatures: Bevis Hillier (Studio Vista)
Mr. Punch's Victorian Era (3 vols): (Bradbury, Agnew)
The Westminster Cartoons (vols 1–5)
Twentieth Century Vol CLXXVIII No 1044.
Drawn and Quartered: ed. Kenneth Pearson (Times Newspapers)

Cartoons by Strube, Cummings and Giles reproduced by kind permission of the *Daily Express*; Illingworth by kind permission of *Associated Newspapers* and *Punch*; Searle, Steadman, Hewison, Partridge by kind permission of *Punch*; Vicky and Jak by kind permission of the *Evening Standard*; David Low by arrangement with the trustees and the *Evening Standard*; Trog and Illingworth by kind permission of *Associated Newspapers*; Dyson, Zec, Whitelaw and Waite by kind permission of *IPC Newspapers*, *Daily Mirror* and *Daily Herald*; Rigby by kind permission of the *Sun*; Birdsall, Heath and Willson by kind permission of the *Spectator*; Lancaster by arrangement with John Murray Ltd and the *Daily Express*.

CONTENTS

We can not unfairly claim to have in Britain the longest unbroken tradition of graphic satire in Europe. That is not to say it is the oldest by any means: the Lutheran (and anti-Lutheran) war of caricatures predated it by two centuries; the boisterous Reformation prints of Holland (which sprang out of the fantastic visions of Bosch and Bruegel and the incisive engravings of Jaques Callot), flooded the English market long before our native artists began to copy them; from Italy our intrepid Grand Tourists brought back the fashionable diversions of emblematic books and the vogue for personal 'caracatura' which Hogarth, purporting to despise, raised far beyond the skills of the aristocratic amateurs.

Nor was this tradition consistently the best in Europe: in France, Daumier and Philipon's publications excelled at a time when the old Gillray tradition in England was running out of inspiration; in the early years of the twentieth century German magazines scintillated with talent while English cartoonists still grappled with the relatively new medium of mass-circulation newspapers. What is unique about the British tradition of cartoons is its freedom of expression, the status almost of a national institution it achieved in this country—in an unbroken progression from the anonymous 'bubble' prints of 1720 to the daily outpourings of the newspaper cartoons of today.

To view history through the eyes of cartoonists is, at the same time, both a puzzling and an illuminating experience. On the one hand they are a vivid and first-hand commentary of our political life. While their fellow artists might be composing their massive and impressive allegories or conjuring up their idealistic or romantic visions, cartoonists took the world and its inhabitants as they were, warts and all (the bigger the warts, come to think of it, the better). Of course, there were those who wanted to make the world a better place: Hogarth whose satires are often infused with a moral tone that would have been more in keeping with (and anyway was an echo of) the Puritan England which was still in living memory; George Cruik-shank with his temperance zeal and genuine horror at social injustices; or Will Dyson with his passionate commitment to the cause of the working class. But it was rarely a high-minded ethic they hawked about, rather it was a grass-roots morality born of Gin Lanes or Jarrows. Indeed it is this close identification with the popular spirit of the times (though here one must except the mid-Victorian cartoonists of *Punch* who were, to a man, the expression of middle-class sentiments) which has been the hallmark, and to some extent the protection, of cartoonists.

For political cartoonists in this country (as many examples in this book demonstrate) have traditionally been granted a licence not tolerated, to this day, in some countries and even here withheld from other kinds of commentators. The publishers of Wilkes or Junius might be hauled before the Bench for their treasonable jottings, theatres closed down for their scurrilous performances and demagogues imprisoned for their hell-raising rhetoric; but cartoonists have continued to heap untrammelled injury on insult, to speak freely with the voice of dissent, radicalism and cynicism.

The milestones in the rich landscape of British political caricature can conveniently be placed at 1720, 1830 and 1890—not turning-points so much as signposts to mark three distinctive stages in the development of cartoons each with a flavour of its own. There is nothing arbitrary in choosing 1720 as the starting-point: that tragi-comic parade of human weaknesses exploited and requited, the South Sea Bubble, heralded the growing public taste for savage invective that was to become characteristic of Georgian society. It inspired a boom in imported (and very quickly home-produced) prints establishing the print-shops as sound commercial propositions, and coincided with the emergence of a competitive and therefore personality conscious parliamentary system of which the first manifestation was the supremacy of Robert Walpole. Throughout the long administration of Walpole (who would have been, if anyone, the man to cut short this licensed abuse in its infancy just as he succeeded in stifling the theatre with a censorship that took over 200 years to shake off) we see the cautious innuendoes of his early years ripening into the specific and highly personal attacks of his vintage. But as the cartoons grew savage enough to do real harm, so Walpole's influence waned too far to do anything about them. His successors in office could scarcely do much, either, about the propaganda they had once revelled in and now found turned against themselves.

By the middle of the eighteenth century the cartoon had matured into a legitimate weapon of political warfare, patronized by Government and Opposition alike and suffered by its victims—not always, let it be said, with any great degree of resentment. It is difficult to believe our political ancestors were any less vain than their modern counterparts who build up large collections of far from flattering caricatures of themselves. Such tolerance did not mean, of course, that the satires were ineffective: Fox, who in his lifetime underwent a barrage of abuse such as few other politicians have had to bear, complained that Sayers's cartoons had cost him more votes than all the speeches in the Commons.

With the exception of certain amateur caricaturists, Bunbury, Darley, Kay and others, who preferred to concentrate on social mannerisms and extravagances, the bulk of artists remained enshrouded in their anonymity, even throughout the American War which provoked an unprecedented onslaught on North's hapless Government as well as on the King. But within a very few years the print-sellers had discovered and cultivated their stables of young 'professional' cartoonists, whose following grew steadily as their originality became known—Thomas Rowlandson, James Gillray, Isaac Cruikshank (and later his sons, Robert and George), Robert Newton, James Sayers, William Heath and many others. These artists represent the high point of English cartoons, a golden age that lasted from approximately 1790 to 1820. The British tradition, although it has displayed many other qualities and talents since, has never equalled these cartoonists of the Napoleonic Wars for sheer vitality or savagery.

By 1830 this rich vein had exhausted itself, its greatest exponents either dead or turned to other work, its public no longer stimulated by the cut-throat politics of a latter-day Pitt or the threat of a new Napoleon. Peace and a surfeit of satire produced a politer, gentler breed of cartoonist like John Doyle, whose lithographs were among the last to be sold separately and Robert Seymour, whose work was published in one of the forerunners of *Punch*. *Punch* itself, after it was established in 1841, epitomized this gentlemanly tradition, making fun of politicians and their policies but rarely giving offence. Such propaganda as remained in cartoons was confined to illegal and underground working-class pamphlets—illegal because they sought to avoid the stamp duty.

For fifty years *Punch*'s great cartoonists monopolized the field: John Leech, Dickie Doyle, John Tenniel, Linley Sambourne. So prolific were they—they also illustrated the works of Thackeray, Lewis Carroll and Kingsley—that it is hard for modern readers to visualize the Victorian age except through their eyes. The challenge, when it came in the nineties, came not from *Punch*'s competitors (though there had been a number of moderately successful rivals, notably *Fun*, *Truth* and *Alley-Sloper*) but from the popular newspapers which had begun to capitalize on the new and rapid developments in printing.

The object of this book is to trace the mainstream of this cartoon tradition and a few of its tributaries, but not primarily from the point of view of the artists' technique nor of their comparative merits. Rather it is to examine the relationship between their work and events—for in the final analysis it is surely by his insight and political effectiveness that a political cartoonist should be judged. Because of this I have no doubt that some readers may think that certain deserving cartoonists have been given a poor deal or that less worthy of their colleagues have obtained too much prominence. But that is in the nature of the book and the strictest criteria I have applied is that of relevance and comprehensibility. I am also aware that the application of the word 'cartoon' to the works of, for instance, Hogarth, is anachronistic. The word itself was, in fact, coined by John Leech and therefore strictly should not be used to describe the great diversity of visual satire in the eighteenth century. I have used 'caricature', 'cartoon', and 'graphic satire' interchangeably, with only the justification that everyone knows a cartoon when they see one.

HOW A POLITICAL CARTOONIST
VIEWS HIS PROFESSION
FOREWORD BY MICHAEL CUMMINGS

In this book the works of the political cartoonist are here for all to see, but what kind of creature, it is often asked, is the man who holds the brush and pen? He is usually regarded as a being who must be slightly eccentric to burden himself with a task that involves the unbearable strain of inventing a constant stream of new ideas.

It is fundamentally a loner's job. The cartoonist is a one-man business. He has to make a white sheet of paper come alive with activity, and he can expect no aid from anyone else.

The first and major daily problem that far transcends the relatively simple task of drawing, is finding the right idea. The cartoonist wakes in the morning and hopes a cartoon-worthy event has happened. If it has, he must digest the happening and form an opinion about it. He must then visualize it into an amusing picture which shows the paradoxical or sardonic aspect—with or without a caption. He allows himself much artistic licence, which is another way of describing caricature. However, I have to say, in the world of today, life is overtaking and surpassing the mere

caricaturist's caricatures. Nowadays there are more and more events of a character so absurd, ludicrous and grotesque that the cartoonist can scarcely make them funnier than they really are. In a world where the human race is developing backwards from adolescence to infancy, the cartoonist gets the sensation of redundancy. Still, though it becomes more difficult for art to improve on nature, the cartoonist soldiers on.

Having plucked his idea from his imagination, he then has the lesser work of drawing it. This straightforward activity may take from two to six hours to complete. This depends on whether he has the simple job of showing a German Emperor dropping the pilot Bismarck (only two figures and a bit of ship) or a Cecil B. de Mille style spectacular of the Labour Party hacking itself to pieces (two days' work and a morning to recover).

Less demanding though the task of drawing may be, compared to idea, it makes a great difference if a cartoonist is master of his pen. A slight idea can be massively entertaining if the drawing is witty and alive, but

"Ah, if only <u>we</u> had black skins..."

10

"Poor chap! He lived before his time!"

Cummings recollects: 'This cartoon on de Gaulle infuriated the French Government and there was an official protest from the Quai d'Orsay to the British Foreign Office. The French Government seemed to think that this cartoon had been "ordered" by the British Government. At the time the usual acrimonious relations between the French and the British were at an all-time boiling point, and this cartoon raised de Gaulle's temperature even higher. This cartoon was reproduced all over the French press, and Paris Match *sent a special correspondent to London to interview me "in depth".'*

a good idea can lose its impact if the drawing is weak or ill composed. Above all, the political cartoonist must be able to make his caricatures instantly recognizable. He must do more than just catch a likeness. His faces must go through the whole range of expression. His 'President' or 'Prime Minister' must be recognizable when smiling, smirking, lying, commiserating, worrying, indignant or simply wearing the mask of sage statesmanship to disguise a total inability to decide what to do next.

To go further, the cartoonist must so dominate his politicians that he can make them recognizable without showing their eyes, nose or mouth. Thus I made a perfectly recognizable drawing of Harold Wilson using such economic means. David Low once made an instantly recognizable drawing of Stanley Baldwin by drawing only his clothes and leaving out his head entirely.

While it is true that there are some public figures whose facial landscape is so richly endowed that one can safely leave out much—like General de Gaulle—there are others whose landmarks are so uneventful that the cartoonist is almost required to invent features to define the man. Such was the case of Selwyn Lloyd. He represented a challenge to us all. This challenge was superbly met, especially by Vicky. Mr Lloyd's face was discreet in general and his nose reticent in particular. But Vicky managed to make of his nose a dominating and commanding feature, by which Mr Lloyd was immediately recognizable. The first time I saw the subject of Vicky's creation, I was astounded by the smallness of his nose—and yet he looked just like the caricature. This is really how we caricaturists must go about our business— we must make the politicians in our image rather than theirs. We must be creators.

Of course, not all politicians require such flights of creative imagination as I have just been describing. Some are almost ready-made caricatures. Adenauer looked like a chunk of the Matterhorn as seen from a Lufthansa Boeing, Kruschev like a snarling billiard ball, Macmillan like an actor playing the part of a Prime Minister in a drawing-room comedy, and Heath like a row of piano keys in a bronzed piano. And so on.

It's often asked if politicians mind being

11

caricatured. In general they seem to like it—or pretend they do—and they frequently ask for the original drawing of the cartoon that has depicted them. I always recall what a Labour cabinet minister said to me many years ago when I was at the beginning of my career: 'Remember, my boy, however angry a politician may be at the way you portray him in your cartoons, he'll be even angrier if you leave him out of your cartoons!'

Not all politicians enjoy being caricatured. On the only occasion I ever met Hugh Gaitskell he regarded me with stunned dismay and distaste. Sir Alec Douglas-Home, by contrast, the first time I met him, spoke energetically about the difficulties of drawing his face and how unsatisfactory the smallness of his chin must be to the caricaturist. Oddly enough, for someone who spends his life drawing rude pictures of public figures, I felt a strange embarrassment at discussing his physical appearance to his face. My subconscious must have been recalling my mother's instruction that it was impolite to make fun of people's physical features.

This brings me to the point that for the good of his professional soul a cartoonist must not get too near his victims or start liking them personally. It takes the edge off your pen if the man whose actions you are about to mock was your generous host of the day before, or the charming and engaging character who sat next to you at lunch.

The cartoonist must remain fundamentally bloody-minded, slightly anarchistic, hold no cows sacred, and must be capable of thoughts in the worst possible taste—but being capable of keeping such thoughts under control when necessary.

While he must always have a point of view about an event—even though it may be wrong-headed—it is sometimes a defect to be too passionate a believer in a certain party or an idea. The cartoonist who succumbs to the dread disease of the Crusading Spirit loses his objectivity. He stands in danger of producing leaden pictures that stun the reader with boredom. The cartoonist should also avoid—like bubonic plague—the 'instant compassion' cartoons shrouded in dark chalk, black clouds and distended corpses. They seldom move or inspire anyone but the artist who drew them.

I must confess, however, that there are

"It's all very well Maudling talking about youth, but I happen to be taking part in an X-certificate film..."

12

"You can't expect the curtain to go up already—I've been playing the overture for only 609 dynamic days!"

times when most of us get a brief rush to the head of the 'crusading spirit'. Very occasionally, a temporary increase of heat under the collar can blast off a dynamic cartoon. Further, if that dynamic cartoon produces shrieks of rage from the victim or victims, summonses to the Press Council or official protests from Quai d'Orsay to Foreign Office, the cartoonist hugs himself with malicious glee. After all, the political cartoonist is a weapon of attack, a warmonger in pictorial aggression. To see his victim writhe ministers to his sense of power.

He well knows that he disposes of an element of power. He can, by constant repetition, create an image of a politician to a large section of the voting public. He can, by his capacity for simplification, encapsulization of a situation and starkness in presentation, produce a shock of prejudice against his chosen target that can be incised on the beholder's mind.

The vivid cartoons in this book are confined to the work of the British cartoonist. The British cartoonist has long enjoyed a singular freedom of expression due to the unique tolerance of all shades of opinion that has prevailed in this country. This is why the British political cartoon has been so vigorous; and it is no coincidence that foreign cartoonists have flocked to Britain to make a living and a reputation for themselves.

Unfortunately, one wonders sometimes if this British tolerance is being somewhat eroded. Witness the intolerance shown by the violent demeanour of the anti-American and anti-Apartheid demonstrators on British streets. Witness the violence of militant students who have broken up lecture-hall meetings addressed by speakers disliked by the militants.

To the political cartoonist, in particular, the most disquieting example of intolerance was when during the power strike the publication of some editions of the *Evening Standard* was stopped because a union disliked the content of a cartoon by Jak.

One hopes that these events are not portents that could mean, if things go ill, that a history of British cartoons for the next two hundred years to come might have less vigour and daring than this history of the last two hundred years of cartoons.

13

I

PRIME MINISTERS

AND THEIR

PARTIES

1721–1742
Robert Walpole, Earl of Orford (Whig)

1742–1743
Spencer Compton, Earl of Wilmington (Whig)

CHAPTER I

English history is littered with Prime Ministers who provided a feast for cartoonists to gorge themselves on. But none offered himself as so succulent a morsel as the very first of their ministerial victims, Robert Walpole. Poor Walpole, so tempting with his bullish features and fleshy twenty stone, and so satisfying in his graceless responses to criticism. It was simply his misfortune that his rise to power coincided with (and doubtless accelerated) the growing popularity of print-shops, which in the first half of the eighteenth century began to purvey a growing range of satires, cartoons and caricatures on the personalities and issues of the day.

While thousands of speculators sank with their worthless companies after the South Sea Bubble, both Walpole and the anonymous breed of cartoonists were carried forward on a tidal wave of popularity—Walpole by his handling of the financial crisis, the cartoonists by their exploitation of it. The very invulnerability of Walpole's position, the initial lack of any organized parliamentary opposition, the security of the King's patronage, all goaded the cartoonists to attack Walpole with a single-mindedness which even the most committed of their descendants would shrink from today. It was an age of unbridled political passions, free from libel laws and censorship; an age of physical politics, with mobs for hire to the highest bidder and disputes resolved by duels where debate had failed (which may explain why so many cartoonists took refuge behind their anonymity). This is reflected in countless contemporary cartoons, where an accurate and detailed observation of the bodily functions was their only claim to merit. But it was also an age of wit and growing sophistication, of Swift and Fielding; this, too, is reflected in many car-

William Hogarth 1697–1764

toons whose mordant humour is still recognizable today.

When, after 1726, an Opposition worthy of the name emerged under Pultney and Bolingbroke they found a ready-made propaganda machine in the ever-increasing flow of prints and lampoons, to which they gave a direction and a purpose. Walpole's party, of course, replied in kind (as did nearly all his successors in office) and with every election or burning parliamentary debate an entertaining war of prints and counter-prints was waged. Cartoonists came to find themselves in the pay of one or other of the political parties (and sometimes both) or of wealthy patrons with a grudge or political ambitions. But the mainstream of Georgian cartoons was anti-ministerial, often quite indiscriminately so, attacking one ministry for doing what they had inveighed against another for not doing.

Under Walpole, however, there was a certain consistency in their targets: the hated standing army of Hessian mercenaries for the defence of Hanover; the Government's appeasing posture towards the diplomatic subtleties of the French and the undisguised aggression of the Spanish, Walpole's own edifice of power built on the manipulation of offices and sinecures, the King's mistresses, the abuses of a corrupt Church, the excesses of the Theatre, and—a happy tradition that has survived in the human interest stories of present-day tabloid papers—a preoccupation with any passing sensation or scandal.

The major satirist of the period was William Hogarth (1697–1764) who produced his first two satires on the aftermath of the South Sea Bubble in 1721, while still working as an assistant to a bookseller. Like much of his early work, they rate as much as social satires as political and indeed a great deal of the work he produced in this period (the *Harlot's Progress, Rake's Progress, Marriage à la Mode,* etc) comes outside the context of this book, however liberally interpreted. The influence, though, of his realistic style and sense of the dramatic on his contemporaries must be acknowledged; and his elevation of caricature into an art-form raised the prestige of a tradition of cartooning which by the end of the century was to become the most admired in Europe.

Even if they never aspired to or attained the heights of Hogarth, his fellow artists slowly abandoned their hieroglyphics, their cryptic or emblematic diagrams and grew more imaginative in their imagery, and, as their effectiveness in the propaganda war increased, more specific in their attacks. John Bull (although invented in 1711) was not to make his début in political prints until mid-century, but other old symbols were adapted and refurbished: Britannia stepped down off her medals and quickly established herself as an enduring favourite with cartoonists, and the British Lion was soon made to endure all manner of indignities at the hands of politicians and his traditional enemy, the Gallic Cock.

One other debt was owed to Hogarth by his fellow engravers. By the 1730s the popularity of political and personal prints had led to the widespread pirating of designs, against which the cartoonist had no legal protection. In 1735 what was dubbed 'Hogarth's Act' secured for them copyright over their engravings and, to some extent, freed them from the exploitation of unscrupulous print-sellers. The Act in no way invested the cartoons with respectability nor curbed their scurrility, but it gave the craft a standing which was to encourage a new and original school of artists.

THE SOUTH SEA BUBBLE

Bubble prints, as they came to be known, were the first popular outbreak of cartoons in England, the seeds from which one of the greatest traditions of satire and caricature in the world was to grow. Even as John Law's infamous Mississippi Company was collapsing in France, cartoonists were arming themselves with a quiverful of sinkable and inflatable imagery. By July 1720 the Privy Council had abolished companies capitalized for such dubious enterprises as discovering perpetual motion and insuring masters against their servants, by September 'almost everybody is ruined who has traded beyond their stock.' And when this rich vein of cupidity and catastrophe was exhausted, the cartoonists were soon looking around for new targets, elated by the success of their bubble prints. Their shafts soon landed on Robert Walpole, whose handling of the crisis had elevated him into a favour with the King he was to enjoy for over twenty years.

1
The South Sea Scheme, Hogarth (1721) Hogarth's first published satire. Directors of the South Sea Company are turning a wheel of fortune, taking subscribers for a ride. The Devil meanwhile hacks away at Fortune's mutilated body, Honesty is broken on the wheel (centre) and Honour is flogged (right).

2
The Lottery, Hogarth (1721) A parody of Raphael's *Disputa* and a satire on the national mania for gambling at National Lotteries (in use since 1694). The lottery is being conducted by Wantonness with her windmill and blindfolded Fortune (right).

3
A Monument of Incredible Folly, Anon (1720) An adaptation of a Dutch original in which Fortune on her chariot scatters shame and beggary to the assembled crowds outside Jonathans (a fashionable coffeeshop). Folly with her hooped petticoats attends her and she is driven by the principal Bubble companies headed by the Mississippi Company with a wooden leg and the South Sea Company with a bandaged leg.

4
The Skreen, Picart (1721) A popular (and recurring) reference to Robert Walpole's reputation for 'screening' the Court from outraged public opinion and an inquiry into its financial dealings during the Bubble. On the screen are depicted Walpole's crimes, behind it lurk the guilty parties including, perhaps, the King's mistress.

1

2

JONATHAN'S

A MONUMENT Dedicated to POSTERITY in commemoration of ye incredible Folly transacted in the YEAR 1720.

Here is represented, Fortune conducted by Folly, who is well known by her ordinary attributes and her
company, who began this pernicious Trade, as ye Mississippi, with a Wooden Leg south Sea with a sore —
of the Dutch West India Assurances India Company are a turning ye Wheel of ye Chariot having
some down, according as ye Wheel turns, with Books of Merchandise crush'd & torn beneath ye Wheel
dvions & Sexes, running after Fortune, to catch ye Actions. In ye Clouds is ye Devil making Bubbles, &c.
which denote ye Besotted, ye Envious and ye Avaricious. Fame flys before spreading every where this
viz.e The Hospitals of Fools, Mad and Beggers. On the Right is ye Man who contriv'd the first
Suppress'd. Those that will give themselves the trouble of cramming ye Print may discover many
the One Young & Laughing, to shew ye best side of the Actions; the other Old and full of Grief, to shew the

Ample Hoop Petticoat, which is also a folly of the Times. The Chair is drawn by the Principal Com-
Leg, and a Ligament upon ye other. The Bank of England treading underfoot a serpent. The Agents
Foxes tails, to shew their Policy & Cunning. On ye Spokes of ye Wheel are seen ye names of several Companys some up
of ye Chariot representing ye destruction of Trade & Commerce, you likewise see a great throng of People as it were
which mingle ne selstions that Fortune distributes to ye Fools Caps which falls to ye lot of some, and ye little serpent
Contagion, those that follow the Chariot are conducted to one of these three Doors, which you see in the Print
Project by setting up a Company at Amsterdam, which was by prudent Foresight of ye Magistrates timely
things, which is not here explain'd that ye curious may have room to guess at. This Folly has for its device Two Heads
contrary. — Just Grav'd 4 Prints upon the Famous ye Stock Jobbing with a List of ye Bubbles by whom each sold & when highest.

A True Picture of the Famous SKREEN describ'd in the Lond.n Journ.l N.o 85

1724–1728

PASSING CONCEITS

In the years following the South Sea Bubble, Walpole proceeded systematically to consolidate his position. Sunderkand, his obvious rival, had conveniently dropped dead in **1722**; the Tories thoroughly discredited by the unmasking of Atterbury's Jacobite plot. High offices in the Church, the Army, State departments, even the Royal Household were filled through Walpole's patronage with friends and supporters—a notable triumph being the dismissal of Lord Carteret as Secretary of State in favour of Newcastle. Apart from skirmishes with Spain over Gibraltar (**1727**), Walpole kept the country at peace and the Opposition at bay, opposition which had consolidated around Bolingbroke (returned from exile and forgiven for his Jacobite sympathies) and Pulteney, and found its voice in the newspaper *The Craftsman*. This faction was soon to rally cartoonists to its cause, but for time being they concentrated more on generalized attacks on corruption or satires on events of a sensational, if passing, interest.

1
Inhabitants of the Moon, Hogarth (1724) This early 'hieroglyphic' print of Hogarth's attacks the venality that was rampant in all spheres of authority, in particular the Court, the Church and the Law. The monarch has a coin for a face, the bishop and the judge are pumping coins into a Church coffer. The King's courtiers are his mirrors (right), his soldiers (left) are his fire-screens.

2
Cunicularii, Hogarth (1726) A famous scandal of the times was the case of Mary Tofts of Godalming. She claimed to have given birth to rabbits and contrived to fool a number of eminent doctors (who travelled from London to witness this remarkable phenomenon) before she was unmasked.

3
Wood Halfpence, Anon (1724) In 1722 a patent was granted to one William Wood (through the good offices, it was said, of the Duchess of Kendal) to produce £108,000 worth of coins for Ireland, where small change was in such short supply that tallies were being used for wages. Such virulent attacks against the whole project appeared over the next two years in Swift's *Drapier's Letters* (castigating it for debasing the Irish currency and as an example of English exploitation of Ireland) that the plan was called off. In the cartoon, the figure of Poverty follows a cartload of Wood's coinage, being driven by devils under the lash of Englishmen.

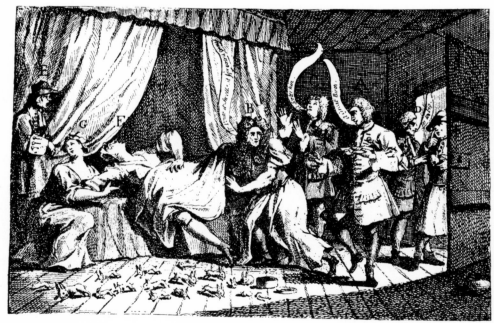

4
Masquerades and Operas, Hogarth (1723) An attack on the decadent state of the theatre. This was the age of Shakespeare tragedies performed with happy endings and Harlequin versions of *Faustus* (a performance of which is packing Drury Lane, right). In the centre a barrow-load of the works of Shakespeare, Dryden, Congreve and Jonson (described as 'waste paper for shops') is being wheeled off.

1729–1735

OPPOSITION TO WALPOLE

Walpole survived his first crisis in 1727 when the source of his power, George I, died. His son was by no means so well disposed towards Walpole as his father and would have had Spencer Compton as his chief minister but for the intervention of the Queen. Seeing Walpole restored to royal favour, the Opposition began in earnest attacking his lavish but carefully-directed patronage, and his pacific attitude towards what were after all our natural maritime rivals, France and Spain (whose Bourbon families were united in a Family Compact against Britain). Soon the Opposition found an influential champion in the Prince of Wales, who displayed what seemed to be the characteristic Hanoverian trait of hating his father. Their first Parliamentary victory came in 1733 with the defeat of Walpole's Excise Bill, against which they contrived to arouse the wrath of the people. It was not enough to unseat Walpole, but, though Bolingbroke retired back to France the next year giving up the unequal struggle, it provided the impetus for renewed attacks on his régime.

1
An Ass loaded with Preferments, Anon (1735) Of all the established hierarchies the one that best fitted into Walpole's system was the Church for it, above all, relied on patronage. In this attack on nepotism the Archbishop of Canterbury drives his ass, the Dean of Canterbury (who also happened to be his son-in-law), loaded with all the gifts over which they have control. Both of them are ignoring the ragged curate at the roadside.

2
Excise in Triumph, Anon (1733) Walpole's Excise Bill (in reality only a duty on wine and tobacco) was made out by the Opposition to be the thin end of a Universal Excise scheme that would impose legions of excise officers on the country. Here Walpole is depicted as one of these excisemen, being drawn by a sour-looking British Lion and his barrel-waggon grinding Magna Carta into the dirt. In the background is the Standing Army, paid for by taxes and loathed by the people, since its prime function was the defence of Hanover.

3
Taste, Hogarth (1731) Matters of taste were the subject of heated controversy in Hogarth's time. This print is a composite of two such controversies of the time: the debate over William Kent's (left foreground) gate for the Piccadilly house of his patron Lord Burlington (on ladder), and a recent attack by Pope (on scaffolding) on the taste of Lord Chandos (in carriage).

AnASS loaded w.th PREFERMENTS

EXCISE IN TRIUMPH

1736-1738

GIN AND MISTRESSES AND FRENCH FLATTERY

The rift between the King and the Prince of Wales widened irreparably in 1737. He removed himself and his wife, bag and baggage, from St James' and set up a rival court at Leicester House. The hopes of the Opposition were still further boosted four months later by the death of Walpole's protectress, Queen Caroline. Soon ambitious patriots were flocking to Leicester House, including William Pitt, whose parliamentary rhetoric became an indispensable asset to the Opposition. Walpole hunted around desperately for a new channel to the King's favour, even importing his favourite mistress from Hanover. It proved to be a futile expedient and as the shadow of Spain darkened the horizon, Walpole's days, he must have known, began to be numbered.

1

Monument to Gin, Vandermijn (1736) One of the more serious social evils of the day was gin, cheap and often lethal. An effort to curb it was made in 1736 with the passing of the Gin Act which imposed a prohibitive tax on the selling of gin. The measure proved quite ineffective, honoured more by breaches of it than by the observance.

2

In Place, Anon (1737) Walpole's relations with France and Spain were the recurring themes of Opposition attacks. Here he is seen, seated at his desk, rejecting the complaints of Captain Jenkins about Spanish atrocities (see next page). Another victim of Spanish depredations is being bundled out of the door, a copy of the Opposition newspaper *The Craftsman* is being burnt, and a Frenchman (Fleury had suspiciously offered to mediate in the Anglo-Spanish dispute) offers jewels to Walpole's wife.

3

Solomon in his Glory, Anon (1738) Until his quarrel with the Prince of Wales, George II had been relatively free from specific cartoon satires. Here, however, he is seen dallying with his favourite mistress, Madame Walmoden, in Hanover. The lady's attentions delayed his return to England for several months.

1

2

SOLOMON in his Glory.
Geo. II.

Come let us take our Fill of Love untill the Morning let us Solace our selves
with Love; For the Good Man is not at Home, He is gone a Long Journey,
He hath taken A Bag of Money with him & will come home at the Day Appointed.
Proverbs 7. 18. 19. 20.
Queen Caroline died 1 Dec. 1737.   19 Dec. 1738
Publish'd According to Act of Parliment Dec: 19 1738

1738–1741

PEACE AND PROVOCATION

Parliamentary opposition to Walpole consistently took the view that his pacific foreign policy was prejudicial to the country's interests. Spain was a case in point. Since 1731, when the Spaniards had cut off the ear of an English sea-captain, Jenkins, for trading in defiance of their monopoly, Walpole had doggedly pursued an almost conciliatory policy. Grievances against Spain had built up and in May 1738 a debate in Parliament urged war against Spain. Walpole delayed declaration of war until late in 1739, once it was clear Spain had no intention of adhering to the terms of the Convention of Pardo. In the election of 1740 the Opposition mounted a bitter propaganda campaign against him, accusing him amongst other things of subservience to France. And when, in October 1740, Maria Theresa acceded to the Hapsburg throne, Philip of Spain's repudiation of her succession, and Britain's support of it, further inflamed the situation.

1
The English Colossus, Anon (1740) An Opposition anti-Walpole print, accusing him of preventing the ships from fighting and ruining trade, of straddling the world like a colossus while '. . . we petty men/walk under his legs and peep about/to find ourselves dishonourable graves'.

2
Slavery, Anon (1738) One of many attacks on Walpole's faint-hearted policy towards Spanish aggression. He is depicted as preventing the British Lion from attacking a Spaniard who drives four Britons in a plough. In the distance a Spanish warship fires broadside at a British vessel, and the luckless Jenkins has his ear removed yet again.

3
French Pacification, or the Queen of Hungary Stript, Anon (1741) Cardinal Fleury, laying most unsanctimonious hands on a blushing Maria Theresa, divides her clothes as spoils to (from l. to r.) Naples, Spain, Bavaria, Poland and Prussia.

1

SLAVERY.

This fortress built by Nature for her self / Against infection and the hand of War, / This happy breed of men this little world, / This precious stone set in the silver sea, / Which serves it in the office of a Wall, / Or as a moat defensive to a House. / Capt. Jenkins, ear cut off by Spaniards, See Smoll Hist / Book 11. chap. 8, 17.

Against the envy of less happy Lands, / This nurse, this teeming womb of royal Kings, / Fear'd for their Breed, & famous for their birth, / Renown'd for their deeds, as far from home. / For christian service and true chivalry. / As is the sepulchre in stubborn Jewry.

Of the world's ransom, blessed Mary's son / This land of such dear souls, this dear dear land, / Dear, for her reputation through the World. / Is now leas'd out, (I die pronouncing it) / Like to a tenement, or pelting farm. / England bound in with the triumphant sea.

Whose rocky shore beats back the envious siege / Of watry Neptune, is bound in with shame, / With inky blots, & rotten parchment bonds.

Shakespeare K. Richard 2.

Publish'd according to a late Act.

To the Worthy and most Injur'd MERCHANTS of Great Britain This Print is most humbly Inscrib'd

Walpole.

1738

F----H Pacification or the Q---N of H-----Y Stript.

With equal hand and a pure heart I share, / The spoils amongst you: For my cost and care

The Countries Love is a reward too poor, / But as you're all my friends, I'll take no more.

Published according to Act of Parliament Feb. 7th 1741/2.

1741–1744

THE FALL OF WALPOLE

By 1741 the Opposition was confident enough for a frontal parliamentary assault on Walpole. In February a motion for his removal was introduced into the Commons amid great excitement and anticipation. This time the Prime Minister rallied and, to the chagrin of the Opposition, obtained a clear majority. But after the dissolution in June, the ensuing election stimulated the propaganda war to new heights, and the rising tide against Walpole was marked by the return of two patriot members for Westminster in the teeth of the Court. His long-delayed downfall finally came in 1742 and was celebrated with glee by the cartoonists, but was also attended by a scramble for power between Wilmington, Carteret, Pelham and Newcastle (from which Pelham emerged in 1744 with the semblance of a stable ministry). The death of Fleury in 1743, moreover, marked the beginning of France's aggressive foreign policy and the substitution of Pitt's warlike slogans for Walpole's appeasing murmurs.

1

The Motley team of state, Anon (1740) An irradiated Walpole is drawn in an ox-cart driven by Lord Hervey the Privy Seal and followed by the Duke of Argyll on a Trojan Horse (bearing gifts of commissions). On the left the Opposition huddles together (Chesterfield, Cobham, Middleton, Pultney, Marlborough and Sandys) disparaging the ill-assorted ministry.

2

The Motion, Anon (1741)   In February the motion for Walpole's removal was defeated in the Commons by 290 votes to 106. This print exults over the disarray of the Opposition after the verdict: Carteret, who inspired the motion, begs to be let out of his coach which is being recklessly driven by Argyll, who supported the motion in the Lords. Sandys (proposer of the motion in the Commons) raises his hands in horror and Pultney with his barrowful of propaganda watches aghast.

3

The Devil upon two sticks, Anon (1741) An election print following the dissolution of George II's third Parliament. Two candidates (left) are seen campaigning and pointing out Walpole having to be carried through a slough of murky policies. Those members who have soiled themselves (right) are those who voted for the 1733 Excise Act and against the Convention of Pardo, by which Spain agreed to pay damages for her maritime depredations.

1

2

THE DEVIL UPON TWO STICKS

To the worthy Electors of Great Britain this Print

on the eve of a General Election

is humbly inscribed and the following Verses are address'd by their Friend & Countryman

Is it not, oh my Friends, a most culpable thing,
To exalt any Villain except in a String?
What then must they be, and how perfectly evil,
With constant supporters who furnish the Devil!
Through Dirt, without Danger, these bear him along
Nor to him the right way is more safe than the wrong —
But I hear a pert Critic, in love with Dispute,
Exclaim' that the Picture & Title don't suit;
Where's the Horns, the cleft foot, & the sad sable hue
That depicture the Devil ad vivum to View?
And then, his Supporters seem rational Creatures!
Have two sticks, you dull Sot, such a shape & such Features?
Be Patient dear Sir, and in brief I reply
That 'tis Belial I'de show by that thing rais'd so high;
And will Horns and cleft feet just Ideas excite
Of the Qualities whilome ascrib'd to that Spright?
He hollow & false wore a specious outside,
And his tongue the designs of his Bosom bely'd;
The worst he could make to appear the best Reason
To dash faithful Council and make it seem Treason,
His thoughts low and mean, still industrious to vice,
Like a Dastard he trembled at honest advice;
So basely averse to each Deed truly great,
He'd advise a lame peace tho' it shackle the State
Or a War so much like it that no one can see
The least mark of distinction between them but he;

Of these bright perfections, that air & that Dress
Are Symbols most proper the World must confess.
These, these in such Colours depicture the Mind
That none can mistake it but those who are blind.
And whoe'er with the share of Attention that's due,
These mystic supporters that bear him shall view,
Must think thus with himself — Matters capis pace
These two things then for certain Imprimis have Place
Man at fire — These are Tools only mov'd by the Devil,
To work his dark purpose and bring about Evil:
Men therefore they are not, yet surely 'twas meant
Thus shap'd and thus dress'd they should Men represent.
That sometimes they should speak but meer Engines we know
Can produce nothing more than a yes or a no —
Now I say the Idea these musings must fix,
Will be that of a Faggot and ergo two Sticks.
But I've done with the Critic — and now oh my Friends!
Fulfill my warm wish that your welfare intends:
The great Now is the time these Supports to withdraw
And three Kingdoms no longer proud Belial shall Awe —
Down, down then at once the great Idol must fall,
And thenceforth be no more than a Dagon or Baal:
For he'l surely expire in that great complication
Of Dirt, which is now call'd the state of the Nation.

* Milton's Paradise lost Book 2d.

a Members who Voted for the Excise & against the Convention
No. 1733. 1739
b Vigourous Measures
c Candidates

9 Jan.

Publish'd according to Act of Parliament January the 9. 1741.

4

The late Prime Minister, Anon (1743)
A gloating print shows Walpole bellowing like a wounded bull at his downfall.

5

The Hanover Bubble, Anon (1743)
Since 1727 Hessian mercenaries had been maintained for the defence of Hanover. They had become a great burden on the taxpayer and the source of much grievance. In spite of attempts to have the standing army reduced there were still 16,000 troops in British pay in 1743. In Parliament Sandwich, Bedford, Chesterfield and Marlborough (amongst those on the right) had spoken out against the army, but the policy of the King (here playing the fashionable game of Tutotum, in which he has just had the winning throw), prevailed.

6

The Pluralist, Anon (1744)   Pluralism, the holding of two or more livings in order to install an underpaid curate in each and live off the income, was one of the major abuses of the Church in Hanoverian England.

THE HANOVER BUBBLE.

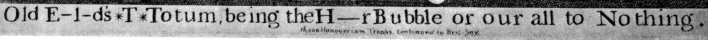

Old E-1-d's *T* Totum, being the H—r Bubble or our all to Nothing.

THE PLURALIST.

II

PRIME MINISTERS AND THEIR PARTIES

1743–1754
Henry Pelham (Whig)

1754–1756
Thomas Pelham-Holles, Duke of Newcastle (Whig)

1756–1757
William Cavendish, Duke of Devonshire (Whig)

1757–1762
Thomas Pelham-Holles, Duke of Newcastle (Whig)

1762–1763
John Stuart, Earl of Bute (Tory)

1763–1765
George Grenville (Tory)

1765–1766
*Charles Watson-Wentworth, Marquess of
Rockingham (Coalition)*

1766–1768
William Pitt, Earl of Chatham (Whig)

1768–1770
Henry Fitzroy, Duke of Grafton (Whig)

1770–1782
Frederick North, Earl of Guilford (Tory)

CHAPTER II

William Hogarth at work

The invasion of Charles Stuart in 1745 unleashed a torrent of bloodcurdling Protestant prints, trying to whip up resistance with visions of the Popish horrors that would be inflicted on the nation should Rome reassert itself once again. The Jacobite response was equally spirited, concentrating on the character demolition of Cumberland, ugly, fat, mean and murderous. Long after the Jacobite scare had died down, cartoons harked back to the Pretender and saw his spectre behind all kinds of unlikely events (the naturalization of Jews, for instance, in 1753 and of course in any weakness towards France). The theme of 'No Popery' was to recur time and time again in the cartoonists' canon, just as Catholic emancipation was later to become a battleground in Parliament.

Although the flame of Opposition guttered with the death of the Prince of Wales in 1751 (throughout the reigns of the Georges the heir to the throne provided a focal point for parliamentary opposition) the cartoonists pursued their theme of ministerial corruption with gusto. With Walpole's monopoly ended and a procession of ministries trooping in and out of office at regular intervals, they had a richer variety of personalities to pillory: the devious Elder Fox, portrayed inevitably but to some purpose as a fox; the luxuriating Newcastle as a goose or an old woman; the comical Lord Bute, kilted (to show off his legs) and preening himself in his rarely-absent boot. Only Pitt, the Elder, escaped their ridicule. The unfortunate Byng, whose surrender of Minorca to the French was seen as indisputable proof of ministerial shadiness, suffered weekly abuse up till his very execution.

Hogarth remained the undisputed master of the art, yet his essays in political satire (up to 1762) continued to be generalized in reference and socially orientated. His Election series begun in 1755 does in fact contain specific allusions and identifiable personalities but is of greater interest as a graphic documentation of contemporary electoral practices. His Invasion prints are sheer chauvinism, inspired no doubt by his treatment at the hands of the French some years before. He consistently turned down overtures—and a great deal of money—to produce anti-ministerial propaganda on commission. Then, quite unexpectedly in 1762, he published a pair of prints that were in substance an attack on Pitt's warmongering and a defence of Bute. This brought down the full weight of Pitt's formidable wrath on Hogarth's head and a blast of personal attacks from rival cartoonists. In vain Hogarth defended himself; within two years he had died brokenhearted.

The bulk of mid-century prints were, like their predecessors, still anonymous though growing in sophistication and beginning to assume a greater political awareness (particularly of the European ramifications) on the part of the buyer. Coloured prints, at double the cost of plain ones, sporadically appeared on the market and the lengthy dissertations, in verse or as quotes from literary authorities, gradually disappeared from the bottom of the cartoons.

The appearance, also, of a number of polemical magazines after 1767—notably the *Political Register*, *Oxford Magazine* and *London Magazine* stimulated a more incisive kind of cartoon, as publishers adopted the fashion of including a few satirical prints in each issue. The magazines themselves soon passed into obscurity, but more enduring was the stimulus they had given to the cartoonists.

1745–1746

THE JACOBITE REBELLION

Cumberland's defence of the Netherlands against France was rudely interrupted in July 1745 by the news of a Jacobite rising in Scotland and the landing of the Young Pretender. By December the Scots had defeated the English army at Prestonpans and advanced as far south as Derby. It was as far as they were to get; in April 1746 a decisive victory by Cumberland at Culloden sent the Pretender hurrying back to France, whence he had come. The war in Europe was not so successful. George II had deserted Maria Theresa and, thinking hopefully of a peace settlement, was outraged by Pitt's bloodthirsty noises. His refusal to have Pitt as Secretary for War brought down Pelham's ministry in February 1746, but Bath and Granville's failure to form an administration restored him to power within days. Pitt, meanwhile, was bought off with a minor office, and the war dragged on.

1

The Invasion or Perkin's Triumph, Anon (1745) A protestant print showing the Popish horrors attendant on a victory for the Pretender (Perkin), whose army by this time had entered England. His carriage is driven by the King of France and the Pope (on the leading horse), the devil rides as footman and an army of Scots follows behind. Britannia is crushed underfoot as the gallows and stake of the Inquisition do their grisly work in the background.

2

The Highland Visitors, Anon (1746) Jacobite invaders descend on an English town, looting and killing. The post-house on the left ('kept by George King') is being stripped of its money.

3

The Butcher, Anon (1746) From his ruthless suppression of Jacobites and Clans after Culloden, Cumberland earned the nickname of Butcher. This Jacobite print constructs a portrait of him from the implements of a butcher's shop (hooks, axe, cleaver, tray, etc), reminiscent of earlier emblematic prints.

4

The Agreeable Contrast, Ebersley (1746) Another Jacobite print comparing the greyhound sleekness of the defeated Pretender with the elephantine lump of Cumberland. Charles Edward receives the admiring glances of Flora Macdonald (who helped him to escape from Scotland); Cumberland is rejected by a whore.

The Invasion or Perkins Triumph. a Protestant Print.

THE HIGHLAND VISITORS.

The Butcher.

5

The Noble Game of Bob Cherry, Anon
(1746) A satire on Bath and Granville's attempts to form a ministry during
the crisis of February 1746. Lord
Granville (Carteret) has had to resign
his secretaryship of state, Lord Bath
(Pulteney) has fallen on the ground in
his attempt to win office, Lord Win-
chelsea is unable to reach and Justice
Willes is running to have his bite at the
cherry with little hope of success. The
outgoing ministry under Pelham (who
returned almost immediately) looks on
in amusement.

4

THE AGREABLE CONTRAST

The Noble Game of Bob Cherry.

1747–1750

FRENCH REVENGE

For another two years the war in Europe went its course with little enthusiasm shown for the policies of the Government and little success for the armies. In 1747 the French invaded Holland and trounced Cumberland at Lauffeldt, the next month the Spanish finally broke the British blockade of Genoa. It was with some relief that, after a false start, Britain finally sat down with France, Spain and the other European powers at Aix-la-Chapelle in 1748 to juggle with their conquests. George II obtained recognition as King of England by the French and received Madras in exchange for Cape Breton Island. But it was the French, the Opposition wryly noted, who emerged from the war considerably richer than they had gone into it.

1
A Country Inn Yard at Election Time, Hogarth (1747)   An election satire inspired by the polling following the dissolution of George II's third Parliament, and in particular the candidature of Viscount Castlemaine as MP for Essex at the age of 20 (hence the baby being chaired, right). His agent, left, is paying the customary bribe to the innkeeper, in spite of the Act against Bribery (a copy of which is in his pocket).

2
The Congress of the Brutes, Anon (1748)   The peace settlement at Aix-la-Chapelle was attacked in customary fashion, notably for ceding Cape Breton Island to the French. The Gallic Cock of France dominates the proceedings with its list of demands. Around the table are: the Lion of Britain and (clockwise) the Eagle of Austria, the Griffin of Germany, the Dog of Genoa, the Leopard of Spain, the Wolf of Prussia, and the Boar of Holland.

3
Locusts, Anon (1848)   In the summer of 1848 there had been an invasion of locusts into Britain, which the cartoonist has used as an excuse for a satire on the predatory nature of the Court and Parliament. The key refers to: 1. Cumberland; 2. Gower, the Privy Seal; 3. Bedford; 4. Newcastle; 5. Pelham, the Chancellor of the Exchequer; 6. the Countess of Yarmouth, one of the King's mistresses; 7. Sandwich.

4
The Roast Beef of England, Hogarth (1748)   After the end of hostilities with France, Hogarth had visited Calais (to do some sketching), where he had been arrested as an English spy. In revenge he drew this satire, where the thin and ragged French soldiers look covetously at a side of beef being delivered to the English eating-house in Calais.

1

2

3

1751–1753

JEWS AND GIN

Momentous events might be happening in the world outside—as indeed they were in India, where Clive was rapidly restoring British fortunes—but little account was taken of them in the print-shops. As so often the cartoonists were preoccupied with domestic matters. Of all the attempts to curb the national vice of gin-drinking during the eighteenth century, the Gin Act of 1751 (whereby the retail of spirits by distillers and shopkeepers was prohibited) proved the most effective. If Hogarth approved of the measure, it cannot be recorded that it was equally popular with all his fellow Londoners. Even less to the public taste was the enlightened legislation of 1753, allowing for the naturalization of Jews in England. Its introduction was greeted with storms of protest and a spate of crudely anti-semitic prints.

1
Gin Lane, Hogarth (1750–51) An unashamedly propaganda production in support of the ministerial measure, showing the evils of gin. Only the pawnbroker and the undertaker are flourishing.

2
A Prospect of the New Jerusalem, Anon (1753) One of a large number of anti-Jewish cartoons which greeted the Naturalization Bill. London has become the Promised Land, the Bill 'a Popish plot to bring in the Pretender' and the Ministry a pawn of the rich Jews.

3
Beer Street, Hogarth (1750–51) The companion print to the above. It depicts ale as a better class of beverage altogether, upon which Trade and Art and Craftsmanship can flourish. The pawnshop, of course, is in ruins.

1

A PROSPECT OF THE NEW JERUSALEM

2

1754–1755

A COUNTRY ELECTION

'There has been such ado with us about election matters that I am ready to die with the vapours; such a rout with their hissing and halloing, my head is ready to split into a thousand pieces . . . Our doors are open to every dirty fellow in the country that is worth forty shillings a year . . . We never sit down to table without a dozen or more boisterous two-legged creatures as rude as bears.' So wrote the wife of a candidate in *The Connoisseur*, on the eve of elections for George II's fifth Parliament. At the same time Hogarth was at work on his Election series, which remains today the most graphic account of the violence, corruption, humour and vitality of eighteenth-century politics.

1
An Election Entertainment, Hogarth (1755) Two Whig candidates are entertaining their supporters at a local inn, while a rival Tory parade passes the window. Some identifiable characters are: the two candidates (left) undergoing the attentions of their social inferiors, the clergyman suffering from an overheated wig, the mayor being bled after a surfeit of oysters (right) and at the door a Methodist refusing a bribe.

2
Canvassing for votes, Hogarth (1755) A voter (centre) is offered bribes by rival innkeepers (party agents). The candidate buys trinkets from a Jew, obviously to gain the attentions of the ladies on the balcony. The inn on the right is a Tory inn, carrying a banner satirizing the Duke of Newcastle; the inn in the distance, being assaulted by a mob, is a Whig establishment.

3
The Polling, Hogarth (1755) The crippled, the dying, the insane and the criminal have been rounded up by both parties. In the background Britannia's coach, unknown to the coachmen, is in danger of collapse.

4
Chairing the member, Hogarth (1755) The victorious Tories are in triumphal procession, the defeated Whigs jeer from a nearby house. Bubb Doddington, later Baron Melcombe, was said to be the model for the member.

1

2

1754–1756

PREPARATIONS FOR WAR

The early months of George II's fifth Parliament saw a frenzy of diplomatic activity. The news from North America was that George Washington was trying to regain the Ohio Valley, which the French, under Duqesne, had seized the year before. Discussions in Paris on colonial boundaries in America foundered; the French ambassador was recalled from London after a British success at the mouth of the St Lawrence (1755). The defence of Hanover was urgently attended to; mercenaries from Hesse and (by the Convention of St Petersburg) from Russia were promised. Austria turned away from its alliance with Britain to a more palatable one with France (1756); Prussia extended the hand of neutrality to Britain, and all in all the only outcome of all this toing and froing could be war, long and expensive. But it was to be Newcastle's war, for Pitt had left the ministry in opposition to the Russian subsidies.

1

The American Moose-deer, Anon (1754)   A company formed in London with exclusive trading rights with the American Indians aroused the jealousy of the local French governors, who continually attempted to encroach on British commerce. In spite of having one of her ships captured by Anson, Spain refused to intervene on France's side. Here, a plump American deer is surrounded by a group of predatory European kings : France feeding it with 'clergy, men, ships, ammunition', etc, Portugal (looking between the horns), Spain (mounted on its back) and George II standing behind with a whip and catching the deers droppings of hides, silk, snuff, etc, in his crown.

2

The Invasion (1), Hogarth (1756) The first of two chauvinistic prints prompted by the outbreak of the Seven Years War. A company of spindly French troops prepare to invade, crying vengeance on 'British beef and British beer'. A monk checks up on instruments of torture that will doubtless be necessary to restore the true faith after the invasion.

3

The Invasion (2) Meanwhile in England the healthy broad-shouldered troops paint graffiti of the French King threatening to 'send my grand Armies and hang you all'. A lad (right) stands on tiptoe in the hope of disguising his youth and being allowed to join up. The inn sign celebrates Cumberland's victory over Catholic forces at Culloden.

1

The American Moose-Deer, or away to the River Ohio.

2

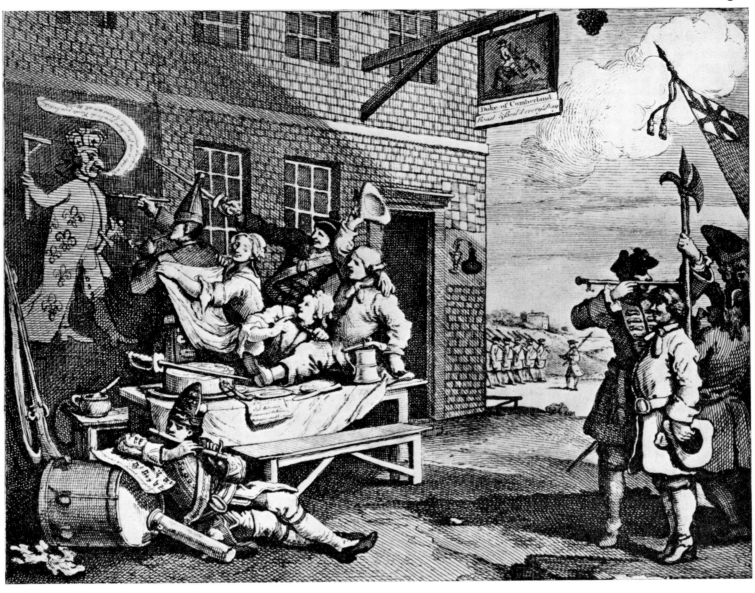

1756–1763

SEVEN YEARS WAR, A BAD BEGINNING

The war with France began disastrously. Almost immediately Admiral Byng surrendered Minorca to the French, and had the mob baying for his blood (and that of the ministers who were accused of selling Minorca to the French). Byng was shot in March 1757, officially for dereliction of duty, in reality as a scapegoat. 'From the clamours of the world', wrote Horace Walpole, 'I was carried away with the multitude in believing he had not done his duty; and in thinking his behaviour, under his circumstances, weak and arrogant, I never interested myself enough about him to enquire whether this opinion was well or ill founded.' Things got worse; Newcastle's ministry fell in November 1756, Devonshire's government collapsed in April 1757, Cumberland (in command of the army in Germany) secured Pitt's resignation, but found himself replaced by George II after surrendering Hanover to Richelieu in September.

1

Birdlime for Bunglers, Anon (1757) Byng lies crushed under a stampede of ministers for money-bait being scattered by a Frenchman. Newcastle (left) holds close his bag of 8,000,000, Fox and Hardwick scrabble for their share, and Anson, the ruined gambler, rushes forward, upsetting a roulette table.

2

The Auction, Anon (1756) The country's assets are being sold off piecemeal to foreign buyers. They include (in the frames on the wall) Hanover, Gibraltar, North America and even the King. The Pretender (right) bemoans the fact that 'I bid for these lots in '45. They are poor now and I suppose will take anything.'

3

Britannia in Distress, Anon (1756) Trade and Publick Credit, the pillars of state, are crushed from above by the weight of pensioned parasites and pulled down from below by the ropes of corrupt ministers.

4

The Sturdy Beggar, Anon (1757) Fox's attempts to form a ministry after the fall of Pitt provided endless material for the cartoonists, as did all his Parliamentary intrigues. This print is a reference to a sinecure held by Bubb Doddington (left) and secured for Fox's sons by reversion.

1

2

1762–1763

BUTE AND THE BEASTS

With the restoration of Pitt's influence at the end of 1757, the tide of war turned. The last three years of George II's reign saw Wolfe scale the Heights of Abraham to take Quebec, Hawke trounce the French at Quiberon Bay, Clive take Plassey and secure Bengal, even the army in Europe win decisively at Minden. The favours of George III, however, coming self-consciously to the throne in 1760, inclined to Lord Bute rather than to Pitt (who resigned as Secretary of State in 1761). Bute, who 'used to pass many hours of every day, as his enemies asserted, occupied in contemplating the symmetry of his own legs', was not popular with anyone else. He was a Scot, which was bad, and he wanted peace, which was worse. And for that he suffered a hail of invective from cartoonists, who seized gleefully on his vanity, his alleged relationship with the King's mother, and the pun on his name. He became then and forever, Boot.

1
The loaded Boot, Anon (1762) makes quite explicit reference to Bute's affair with the Princess of Wales. A horse and a zebra (the King and Queen) are led by Fox, and the whole contraption is admired by ambitious Scotsmen.

2
The Times (*1*), Hogarth (1762) An exception among cartoonists was Hogarth, who made two ill-starred attempts to support Bute's ministry against the warlike policies of Pitt. A fireman from the Union Office (i.e. between England and Scotland) tries to extinguish a fire engulfing the globe. Pitt, in the guise of Henry VIII, fans the flames; his supporters meanwhile set up shop opposite, erecting signs that display their internal dissensions.

3
The Times (*2*) shows the well-tended garden of government as Bute would have it. Pitt's party continues to fire at the dove of peace, the Lords are bored by it all, the crippled of the Seven Years War are shut out and Wilkes (right) gets his deserts.

4
The Hungry Mob of Scribblers and Etchers, Anon (1763) Hogarth himself suffered from his Butite propaganda. Here he is shown (with engraving tool), along with Samuel Johnson holding his pension and Smollett, all receiving hand-outs from Bute.

5
The State Quack, Anon (1762) Bute poses as a quack doctor with his union-syringe 'to mend the constitution'. The Princess of Wales dances on a tight-rope, balancing a boot on her midriff.

48

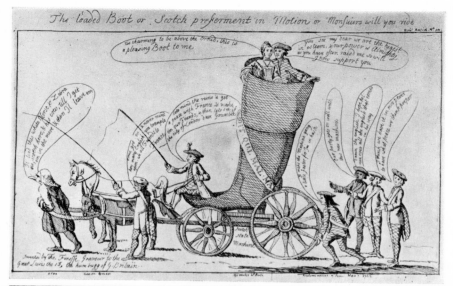

The State QUACK

1762–1765

THE TROUBLE WITH WILKES

The torrent of anti-Bute invective had its effect in April 1763, when he resigned in favour of Grenville (though he continued for some years, in the cartoonists' canon, to be a symbol of 'royal influence'). One of his bitterest lampooners had been John Wilkes in his newspaper *The North Briton*; now Wilkes turned on the King. He denounced the Peace of Paris (which ended the Seven Years War in 1763) and added in issue 45 that he hoped the King would not profane St Paul's by attending a thanksgiving service there. Halifax, the Secretary of State, at once had him arrested for seditious libel, but Mr Justice Pratt (who, like Wilkes, was of Pitt's faction) discharged him on grounds of Parliamentary privilege. Wilkes retaliated by suing Halifax for damage to his property, and won. From that moment, Wilkes became the hero of the common man, his name synonymous with Liberty. When he was expelled from the Commons and fled to France, there were riots in London. But neither London, nor the King, had heard the last of him by any means.

1
An Exciseman, Anon (1763) An oblique attack on Bute for the introduction of a Cider Tax in his budget of 1763, echoing the widespread fears of a general excise in 1733. Symbols of other necessities of life taxed at that time are included: land, candles (arms), leather (breeches), beer, tea and coffee (right and left) and windows (setting sun).

2
The Pillory Triumphant, Anon (1765) John Williams, printer of *The North Briton*, reissued no. 45 after Parliament had ordered it to be burnt. His punishment was pillorying in Palace Yard, but here the crowd just shout 'Sons of Wilkes and Liberty!' The ubiquitous Boot reappears, this time on an improvised gibbet.

3
John Wilkes, Esqr, Hogarth (1763) The staff and cap of Liberty are sarcastic references. Wilkes himself (in Hogarth's words) possessed a face that was 'so arrant a Joke that it set everybody else a laughing'.

1

1765–1768
RESISTANCE IN AMERICA

Even in the backwoods of America the cry 'Wilkes and Liberty' could be heard. The French menace may have been diverted in Europe, but it was still very real on the Mississippi; the patronizing attitude of British administrators served only to convince colonists that London was intent on taxing them white to pay for a war that was not over for them. Grenville's ill-timed Stamp Act of 1765 was the last straw. Nine colonies met in New York to draw up a declaration of their rights and liberties. In the public mind in Britain, the colonies and Wilkes became inextricably mixed, and in deference Rockingham's brief ministry (1765–66) repealed the Act, but reiterated Parliament's right to tax the colonies. As indeed it proceeded to do the following year under the new Grafton-Pitt (now Lord Chatham) régime. Tea, glass, paper and dyestuffs all were taxed to provide revenue for colonial administration. The resistance in America focused on Massachusetts, where the Assembly was dissolved (1768) for refusing to assist in the collection of taxes and the citizens of Boston rioted.

1

The Deplorable State of America, Anon (1765) Britannia is offering Pandora's Box (Stamp Act) to America, here as so often later on depicted as an Indian. Liberty is prostrated and Mercury (commerce) flies away. The King of France offers a bribe to (what else?) a hovering Boot.

2

The Repeal or the Funeral of Miss Ame-Stamp, Benjamin Wilson (1766) Known to have been officially inspired by Rockingham's ministry. The funeral procession is led by Grenville (holding coffin), with Bute as chief mourner. On the tomb is inscribed a long list of iniquities which 'tended to alienate the affections of Englishmen to their country', including Excise Money and General Warrants. A space is left for Miss Ame-Stamp.

3

The Colossus, Anon (1767) A rare anti-Pitt cartoon, inveighing against his denunciation of the Stamp Act. One of his stilts (Sedition) hangs over New York, the other (Popularity) is firmly ensconced in the City.

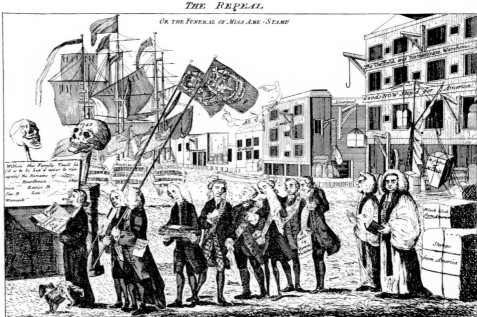

4

The Colonies Reduced and Its Companion, Anon (1768) In the first, Britannia has slipped from her globe, mutilated of her colonial limbs. In the second, Bute has exposed America to Spain and forced her into the arms of France. A Dutchman, meanwhile, runs off with her shipping.

5

The Funeral of Freedom, Anon (1769) In spite of being expelled from Parliament Wilkes was returned three times by the electors of Middlesex in rapid succession. At the third attempt Parliament in desperation declared the elections illegal and seated his opponent, Colonel Luttrell. In the riots that followed this decision two men (named Clarke and Allen) were killed and immediately became martyrs in the cause of freedom. At the foot of their tombs (left and right) and Wilkes's (centre) lie the heads of Cromwell and Charles I. Accompanied by the devil, on the left, stand Bute, Grafton and Lord Holland, with Viscount Weymouth (who suppressed the Wilkite riots) brandishing his sword.

1770–1772

THE KING'S INFLUENCE

For the two years in which he and the voters of Middlesex defied the authority of Parliament, Wilkes had been the cartoonists' dream. From 1770 he faded rapidly from the public consciousness, his function as thorn-in-the-side of Parliament and King appropriated by the pamphleteer Junius, whose publishers were tried in 1770 for seditious libel. With the emergence of Lord North as Prime Minister after Grafton's resignation in 1770, the King laid himself open to a public scrutiny unprecedented among the Hanoverians. North was no Walpole; the hallmark of his administration was complete acquiescence in the King's will, his ministry was dubbed the King's Friends. Previous Georges might have been twitted for being German or keeping mistresses: George III was openly (and somewhat unfairly) abused for neglecting affairs of state.

1

The Button-makers adjusting their differences, Anon (1770) George III is accused of selling out to Spain over the question of the Falkland Islands—invaded earlier in the year by the Spanish governor of Buenos Aires. Spain ceded the islands to Britain the next year, but refused to pay reparations. Button-making was popularly believed to be the King's favourite hobby.

2

The Vicar Purified by the Shadow of Junius, Anon (1771) A quarrel between Wilkes and his supporter the Rev Horne-Tooke (who was later to open a fund for the American colonists) was waged in public. The brilliant and anonymous political commentator Junius suggested that Tooke had been put up to this quarrel by ministers.

3

Farmer George studying the wind and weather, Anon (1771) A specific attack on the King's alleged neglect of his public duties.

4

The Young Politician, Anon (1771) The introduction of Charles Fox into political cartoons. He is being coiffured by two French hairdressers in the style of a Macaroni (predecessor of the Dandy). In his hands is a torn-up copy of Magna Carta—a reference to his rigid opposition to Wilkes, and therefore to liberty.

5

Picture of Europe for July 1772, Anon The King slumbers on his throne, while Austria, Russia and Prussia engineer the Partition of Poland between them, and Britain's influence in Europe wanes.

The Button Makers adjusting their Differences.

THE VICAR PURIFI'D BY THE SHADOW OF JUNIUS.
Rev.d I. Horne Tooke
Pub.d accord.g to Act of Parl.t Aug.y 7.th 1771 by M.Darly 39 Strand.

Farmer G—e, Studying the Wind & Weather.

C.J.Fox.

THE YOUNG POLITICIAN

Publish'd accor.te Act by H. Bryer London.

1773-1774

KING AND COLONIES

On the subject of the American colonies the King would countenance no compromise whatsoever; the colonists had threatened secession, burnt his ships, established treasonable committees and in December 1773 had tipped his tea into Boston harbour. The Americans' petition to have the Governor-General of Massachusetts removed went unheard; instead Parliament obediently passed Coercive Acts against the colony, which included the closing down of the port of Boston, and took the precaution of passing the Quebec Bill to ensure Canada's loyalty (by establishing Roman Catholicism and law in Canada) should it come to war (1774). The colonists replied in kind, resolving to ignore the coercive legislation and voting (at their first Continental Congress at Philadelphia) to ban all imports from Britain. War was now inevitable.

1

The Mitred Minuet, Anon (1774) To the music of Bute and the Devil and to the approval of North, bishops dance at the passing of the Quebec Bill—intended to secure the loyalty of French Canadians before a possible American war, but reviled in Britain as a stage in the further encroachment of popery.

2

The Present Times, Anon (1773) In 1772 Clive had successfully defended his administration in Bengal in the House of Commons. Nevertheless a Regulating Act was passed in May 1773 setting up a Council to veto, if necessary, the acts of the Governor-General. Here Clive and Colbroke are seen handing over their 'hush-money' at pistol-point to North, while Bute distracts the course of justice.

3

America in flames, Anon (1774) Lord North peers through his lorgnette in approval as Bute and Thurlow (in his Chancellor's robes) fan the flames of America with their repressive legislation. A group of patriots try vainly to extinguish the conflagration. The Boston Tea Party, the spark that set the fire alight, is represented by a teapot tumbling down the steps.

4

The Devil turn'd fortune-teller, Terry (1774) America appears in a vision (all too prophetic) to Lord North, in which the British Army is prostrated and Parliament emptied of its miniature inhabitants.

5

The Mother and Child, Anon (1773) The King appeals to a distinctly haggard Britannia for more supplies to effect his designs on the recalcitrant colonists.

56

1

The Mitred Minuet.

A New Scene for the Proprietors of India Stock

The Present times, or the Nabobs CL-VE and C-L-KE brought to Account

2

3

Delign'd & Engrav'd by G. Terry,

Pater noster Row

The Parl^mnt. diſſolvd, or,
The DEVIL turn'd FORTUNE TELLER.

Privy Purse in 1753.

Jan. Lond.Mag. 1773.

Privy Purse in 1773.

GR III

GEO. III.

The Mother and the Child.

1774–1776

THE BOSTON TEA PARTY AND AFTER

Obsessive though the eighteenth century cartoonists were, few events stimulated and possessed them as thoroughly as the American War of Independence. From the Boston Tea Party in December 1773 onwards, they threw themselves into producing a torrent of anti-Government satires. They railed at the Coercive Acts against Massachusetts, reviled the closing of Boston's port and ridiculed the retreat from Concord to Lexington. Chatham's efforts in February 1775 to introduce legislation conciliatory to the colonists was thrown out of Parliament and replaced by more repressive measures. Grafton's protest-resignation was accepted with equanimity. On the other side of the Atlantic, the colonists organized themselves for a war they knew Britain couldn't win: George Washington was appointed commander-in-chief, and at the Philadelphia Congress under John Hancock they set out their war aims.

1

The Able Doctor, Anon (1774) Under the gloating gaze of the Kings of France and Spain (left), North forces a potion from a teapot down the throat of America, aided by Bute (holding a sword), Mansfield and Sandwich. Britannia weeps and in the distance British ships bombard Boston.

2

Six-pence a day, Anon (1775) An attack on recruiting for the American war. The horrors of a soldier's life at sixpence a day are contrasted with the comforts of a chairman's life, at three shillings a day, a driver's at two shillings and even a sweep's boy at a shilling a day.

3

The Parricide, Anon (1776) A rare gleam of comfort for the Ministry. America, as an Indian, attacks Britannia, whose arms are pinioned by patriots including Chatham and Fox. The attack is being encouraged by Wilkes (centre).

4

Noddle Island, Darly (1776) Matthew Darly specialized in satirizing the extravagant hair-styles of the day, which were so enormous that he could envisage all manner of events occurring on them. Here the battle for Boston is taking place, in which Washington forced the British troops under Howe to evacuate the city.

The able Doctor, or America Swallowing the Bitter Draught.

The Parricide.

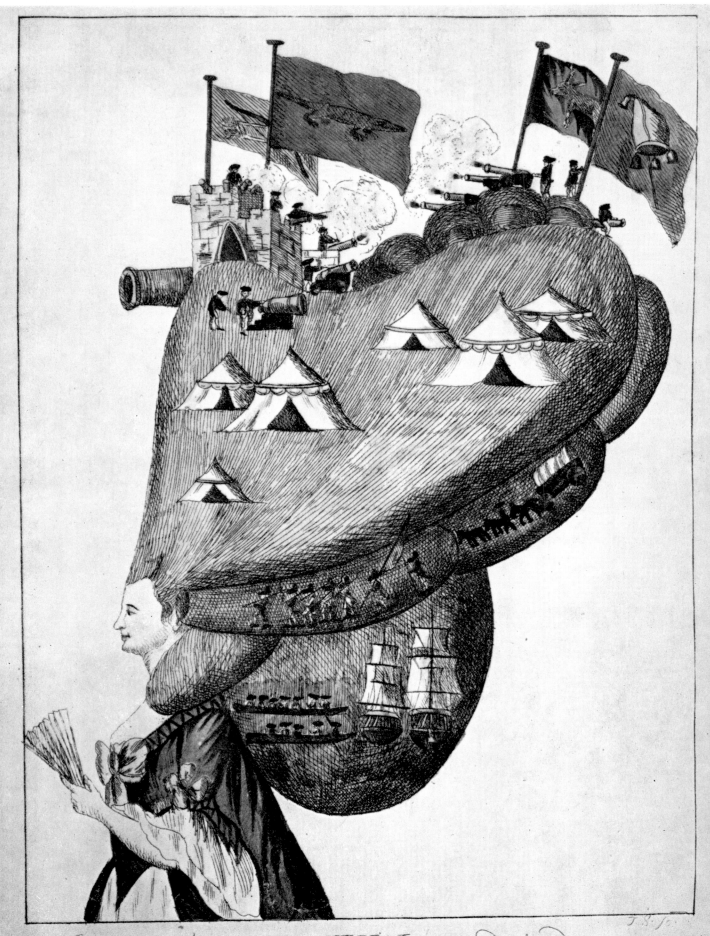

NODDLE·ISLAND· or HOW· are we deciewed.

CHAPTER

III

PRIME MINISTERS
AND THEIR
PARTIES

1770–1782
Frederick North, Earl of Guilford (Tory)

1782
Charles Watson-Wentworth, Marquess of Rockingham
(Whig)

1782–1783
William Petty, Earl of Shelburne (Whig)

1783
William Bentinck, Duke of Portland (Coalition)

1783–1801
William Pitt the Younger (Tory)

CHAPTER III

James Gillray

Thomas Rowlandson

The momentous events and colourful personalities of the last quarter of the eighteenth century happily coincided with the emergence of a group of brilliant and original cartoonists. The combination was to produce a Golden Age of cartoons which lasted till well after the end of the Napoleonic Wars. The unpopularity, not to say the humiliations, of the American War united the cartoonists in a concerted barrage on the King and his puppet ministers. Barely a handful of prints came to their aid. Lord North never recovered from the attacks, though the King slowly returned to favour after the war was over. Partly it was sympathy for his derangement, partly horror at the excesses of republicanism in France and very largely the behaviour of the Prince Regent, whose debts, morals, and associates made him a riper plum to be picked.

In the late eighties the prints are dominated by William Pitt (the Younger) and Charles James Fox, whose struggle for power and rhetorical duels were the highlight of Georgian politics. Both had their supporters among the cartoonists, but it has to be admitted that Fox came off worse if only because of the intervention of Gillray (himself no Pittite but a relentless pursuer of Fox). Pitt, in common with his predecessors Walpole, Bute and North, was accused of 'secret influence' at Court and later of attempting to usurp the power of the monarchy. Fox, on the other hand, was the dangerous radical, a tool of Jacobins, Irishmen and revolutionaries, a republican and threat to the established order.

Initial sympathy for the French Revolution in the cartoons soon turned to repugnance, which vented itself on self-confessed supporters of the revolution ('the patriots') Priestley and, even more savagely, Tom Paine, whose absence from the country was no protection whatever. Where once the cartoonists had made the broad distinctions between Court and Opposition, Corruption and Patriotism, the 'patriots' now became a thoroughly disreputable bunch and as corrupt as any administration.

The front rank of the new professional cartoonists was occupied by James Gillray (1757–1815) and Thomas Rowlandson (1756–1827). Gillray's work was essentially non-partisan, conditioned by his staunch patriotism and his abomination of all things Catholic or French, and by his upbringing among the Moravian Brethren whose gloomy faith was pinned on the basic depravity of man. He was a product of the Royal Academy schools where he studied under Bartolozzi the Italian engraver, and after entered into partnership with the most famous print-publisher of the time, Hannah Humphrey, whose well-ordered establishment ran off Gillray's designs at high speed and at considerably less cost. Gillray had his prejudices, notably Fox, Burke and Sheridan, but until he was awarded a pension by the Government in 1797 his wit and dis-

respect ranged over the political spectrum.

Thomas Rowlandson, too, was a pupil of the Royal Academy schools and gained a reputation as a portraitist. His conversion to satire and caricature was less from political motives than financial, to pay his enormous gambling debts. Like Hogarth his most famous work was primarily social (his Dr Syntax series was the forerunner of the modern strip cartoon) and his disinterest in politics is illustrated by the fact that his most effective political satires are developments of other people's ideas—in particular of George Woodward, whose good-humoured sketches were well suited to Rowlandson's mocking but refined style.

Among the many other active and influential cartoonists was James Sayers (1748–1823), a lawyer by profession and known to have been in the pay of the Treasury. His soft-ground etchings were committed Pittite productions for which he was rewarded with a lucrative sinecure in 1786. Nor was it only the cartoonists who prospered—the print-shops became an indispensable part of everyday life offering morning lounges to patrons, exhibitions and folios for hire. As well as Hannah Humphrey's shop in Bond Street, Fores opened in Piccadilly, Hollands in Drury Lane and Ackermanns in the Strand, each one becoming a traditional visiting-place for any gentleman of taste who wished to keep abreast of current affairs.

1777–1779

NO QUARTER

With every year of the war, the King's resolve became more entrenched. Grafton's peace moves in 1776 foundered, the Rockingham Whigs' protests went unheeded and Chatham denounced the war to his dying breath in 1778. North, too, would gladly have put an end to the affair, but he was a creature of the King. His proposals for reconciliation in February 1778 and the appointment of Commissioners to negotiate with Congress came too late. They might have succeeded but barely a fortnight before France had signed an offensive alliance with the colonists and were not to be robbed of their war. In June Congress rejected the peace offer. Worse was to come. The next year Spain, encouraged by the French offer of support, declared war and began a siege of Gibraltar that was to last four years. There was talk, even, of an invasion with the French fleet utterly dominating the Channel.

1
Review of the York Regiment, Anon (1777–8) An attack on the support the war was getting from sections of the Church, and in particular the Archbishop of York (centre). 'For mitre, deaneries and prebendarys', says the leader of the cleric-troop, 'we will wade through an ocean of Yankee blood.'

2
A Picturesque View of the State of the Nation for February 1778, Anon North's conciliatory proposals alarmed the Opposition, who applied some convoluted logic to denounce them, as in this print. British commerce (the cow) is being mutilated by America and milked by the Dutch, Spanish and French. Meanwhile the Lion sleeps, British admirals idle away their time and an honest Englishman is in despair. North's proposals, it was argued, were evidence of the general apathy.

3
The Liberty of the Subject, Gillray (1779) With the war devouring manpower and an imminent invasion threatened, press-gangs were a grim feature of daily life.

4
Who's in fault? Anon (1779) The Navy's failure to control the Channel had to be laid at someone's door and it landed at Admiral Keppel's, who had been court-martialled for failing to attack at Ushant in July 1778. He was acquitted, but was for ever compared unfavourably with the dashing Rodney. 'The anatomists will have it', reads the caption, 'that it can have no Heart having no Body—but the Naturalists think if it has a Heart, it must lay in its Breeches.'

Review of the York Regiment.

Westm. Mag. Feb. 1776

A Picturesque View of the State of the Nation for February 1778.

1779–1780

PRESSURE ON PARLIAMENT

Widespread frustration with the King's intransigence and his coterie of friends and counsellors began to express itself forcibly in Parliament and the country. In February 1780 a Yorkshire petition for Parliamentary reform was presented at Westminster, and two months later Dunning proposed a resolution deploring the increased influence of the Crown. The principle of a periodic scrutiny of the Civil List was subsequently adopted in the Commons, and in May a further erosion of the King's influence was pressed by Burke's introduction of a Bill for economic reform, aiming, among other things, at the abolition of sinecures and redundant offices. The war ground on, with enough British victories (Rodney at Cape St Vincent and Cornwallis at Horatio Gates) to enable North to cling to power, and enough reverses to encourage the cartoonists to step up their campaign.

1
The Horse America throwing his Master, Anon (1779)   A dire prophecy of ultimate defeat for the King's policy. A Frenchman runs to take over the riderless horse.

2
The State Tinkers, Gillray (1780)   An attack on the King's supposed subversion of the Constitution (the State kettle). George III, portrayed as a despotic sultan, looks on in pleasure as North and his cronies tinker with the bowl.

3
The French Spy, Colley (1780)   Britain was at war with France, but the Frenchified fashions of the decade lingered on. They were soon to give way to the plainer attire of the '80s.

4
The Allies, Anon (1780)   In 1779 Congress had had to send troops into the Wyoming Valley as reprisals against Indian attacks on Pennsylvania. Here the Indians are represented as the allies of George III and enjoying a cannibalistic meal of the bones of colonists with him—with the blessing of the Church, or at least the Archbishop of York.

1

THE HORSE AMERICA, throwing his Master.

2

THE STATE TINKERS.

The National Kettle, which once was a good one, / For boiling of Mutton, of Beef, & of Pudding, / By the fault of the Cook, was quite out of repair, / When the Tinkers were sent for, ___ Behold them & Stare.

The Master he thinks, they are wonderful Clever, / And cries out in raptures, 'tis done! now or never! / Yet sneering the Tinkers their old Trade pursue, / In stopping of one Hole ___ they're sure to make Two.

Publish'd Feb.y 10th 1780. by W.Humphrey N° 227 Strand.

The FRENCH SPY,
taken Prisoner by English Girls.

THE ALLIES.— Par nobile fratrum!

The Party of Savages went out
with Orders not to spare Man
Woman, or Child. To this cruel
Mandate even some of the Savages
made an Objection, respecting the
butchering the Women & Children,
but they were told the Children
would make Soldiers, & the
Women would keep up the
Stock.

Remembrancer Vol. 8, p. 77

Qui facit per alium, facit per se.

1780–1781

PROTESTANTS AND PROFITEERS

Rodney's successes may have given North's ministry another eighteen months of life, but they were not happy ones. Disgust at the Catholic Relief Bill of 1778 which had been fermenting for a year into agitation for its repeal, exploded in June 1780 into organized violence. Catholic chapels were pillaged and a procession to petition Parliament (headed by Lord George Gordon) developed into a riot in London. The Irish, too, took the opportunity of Britain's preoccupation in America to air their grievances. In April 1780 Henry Grattan pressed his demands for Home Rule. In December he won his battle for the abolition of Irish trading restrictions, but no hint of self-government. Two years later, after the fall of North, he tried again by formulating an American-style Declaration of Rights and demanding legislative freedom. This time he found allies in Shelburne and Fox whose Repeal of the Ireland Act won the legislative independence Grattan wanted. But it was a Pyrrhic victory, for his Parliament was elected solely by Protestants.

1
No Popery, Anon (1780) Many cartoons, such as this, were published whitewashing the role played by Protestants in the Gordon riots. The looting and the damage (the implication is) was the work of ruffians or Catholics masquerading as petitioners.

2
Malagrida and conspirators, Gillray (1782) Grattan's demands for Irish Home Rule found a sympathetic audience in the Whig coalition and especially in Shelburne (Malagrida) who was himself a Jesuit.

3
The Coffee-House Patriots, Bunbury (1781) St Eustatius in the Dutch West Indies was an important supply-base for the American colonists and also, it was believed, a centre for illegal British trading with the enemy. Here such profiteers read of the news of its capture by Rodney with grim faces.

4
A Chop House, Bunbury (1781) Boswell and Dr Johnson at work on a snack.

NO POPERY or NEWGATE REFORMER.

Tho' He says he's a Protestant, look at the Print,
The Face and the Bludgeon, will give you a hint,
Religion he cries, in hopes to deceive,
While his practice is only to burn and to thieve.

MALAGRIDA & Conspirators, consulting the Ghost of OLIVER CROMWELL.

3

69

4

1782

THE KING IN A CORNER

North's resignation in March 1782 and the Whig coalition of Rockingham, Fox, Burke and Shelburne, which took his place, put the King in a tight situation. They were his enemies and an end to the war was inevitable. 'His Majesty', he wrote in a letter, 'is convinced that the sudden change of sentiments of one branch of the legislature has totally incapacitated him from either conducting the war with effect, or from obtaining any peace but on conditions which would prove destructive to the commerce as well as essential rights of the British nation.' The death of Rockingham in July and the substitution of the Shelburne-Pitt ministry was no better. He regarded himself as the prisoner of his ministers; he disliked the economies of Burke's Reform Bills, and he viewed Fox's efforts to have the Prime Minister elected by the Cabinet (an attempt to keep out his inveterate enemy, Shelburne) as the undermining of constitutional monarchy. He even contemplated abdication.

1
The Captive Prince, Gillray (1782) From right to left: Rockingham ('Dispose of these jewels for the public use'), Cavendish and Richmond ('I command the ordnance'), The King ('Oh, my misguided people'), Keppel ('I command the fleet'), Fox ('I command the mob'), Conway ('Which way shall I turn, how can I decide?') and Burke ('The best of ministers, the best of K . . .').

2
Britannia's Assassination, Gillray (1782) A mob of patriots, including Fox, Wilkes, Dunning and Keppel, dismember Britannia on her globe. Two judges (Thurlow and Mansfield) try to protect her, while Holland, Spain and America make off with her parts. Empty-handed France pursues America.

3
Gloria Mundi, Gillray (1782) Fox, bestriding a globe and a roulette wheel, berates the rising sun of Shelburne. Fox's gamble to keep Shelburne out of office failed, and along with Burke he was excluded from the new ministry.

1

2

GLORIA MUNDI,

or — The Devil addressing the Sun. *Par: Lost. Book IV.*

C.J. FOX

L.D. Shelburn.

1782–1783

FOX GOING TOO FAR

The inevitable peace came in 1783 at Versailles, with Britain recognizing the independence of America. But not before Shelburne had resigned after a resolution censuring the peace preliminaries. In April the Duke of Portland emerged as the nominal premier of what was in reality a Fox–North coalition. Fox's political activity in these two years was phenomenal. In 1782 he had gained a striking success with his repeal of the Ireland Act (though Grattan's Parliament was elected solely by Protestants). In December 1783, he overplayed his hand with the introduction of his India Bill, by which the Commissioners who were to govern India were to be appointed by Parliament not the Crown. This was too much for George III. He persuaded the Lords to throw out the Bill, and the next day fired the Coalition.

1
The Blessings of Peace, Anon (1783) The King (centre) appeals to his ministers 'My Lords and Gentlemen, what shall I do?' In reply he gets evasive answers, as from North (front right) 'I thought to have had America at our feet, but I see 'tis otherwise', and categorical as from Fox (front left) 'Keep Peace on any terms'. On the other side of the Atlantic, Spain, France and Benjamin Franklin are more interested in courting the favours of America.

2
A Transfer of East India Stock, Sayers (1783) With India House on his shoulders Fox carries off patronage from the Crown to the Coalition.

3
Carlo Khan's triumphal Entry into Leadenhall Street, Sayers (1783) Carlo Khan, as Fox came popularly to be known, rides his India Bill (with the face of North and led by Burke) into the City. The banner reads King of Kings, in Greek—an echo perhaps of Alexander the Great.

1

2

Carlo Khan's triumphal Entry into Leadenhall Street.

1784

THE RISE OF PITT

The King's invitation to William Pitt to form a ministry was a gamble. At the close of 1783, Pitt was the sole member of the Cabinet in the Commons; there were many and powerful factions ranged against him. But he was an ambitious and independent man who would stride through the Chamber 'looking neither to the right nor to the left; nor favouring with a nod or a glance any of the individuals seated on either side, among whom many who possessed five thousand a year'. His instinct for survival drew a steady trickle of support to his side until, in March 1784, the opposition to him had dwindled to a majority of one, and in the subsequent election he gained a sweeping majority. From that time on Fox, who only scraped home in a cliff-hanger of an election at Westminster, forgave neither Pitt nor the King.

1
The Covent Garden Night Mare, Rowlandson (1784) A parody of a painting by Fuseli recently exhibited at the Royal Academy. Fox dreams of defeat in his election campaign at Westminster, where at one stage his rival Sir Cecil Wray looked like gaining an overwhelming victory. The tide of his fortunes, it was said, was turned by the frenetic canvassing of the Duchess of Devonshire, who drove electors to the polls in her own carriage.

2
The Battle of the Umbrellas, Collings (1784) As the excesses of the Macaroni styles for men died out so women turned to the monstrosities of the Derrière. By the middle of the '80s umbrellas were very much in fashion for both sexes.

3
Britannia Roused, Rowlandson (1784) In her anger at the Coalition, Britannia hurls Fox and North to the ground.

1

THE COVENT GARDEN NIGHT MARE.

2

BRITTANNIA ROUSED,
OR THE COALITION MONSTERS DESTROYED

Rowlandson

4

The British Titans, Anon (1784)
George III (as Jove) hurls Fox down
into the abyss to join (left to right),
Burke, Cavendish and North. On the
Olympian heights stands an irradiated
Pitt, crowned with the victor's laurel
leaves.

5

The Infant Hercules, Anon (1784)
Ensconced on the shield of Chatham a
baby Hercules (probably Pitt himself)
strangles the serpents Fox and North
(whose tails are inscribed with their
respective political failures, the East
India Bill and the American War).

4

First 'Typhon strove more daring than the rest,
With impious hands the imperial Bolts to wrest:
Nov. 22, 1784.

THE BRITISH
TITANS.

Him and his Crew the red right arm of Jove,
Down to their native Hell indignant drove,

1785–1786

PUBLIC SCANDALS

Wars, elections and Cabinet crises over for the time being, the cartoonists turned to other, no less intriguing, topics. There was, for instance, the clandestine marriage of the Prince of Wales to Mrs Fitzherbert in December 1785. This, together with rumours of orgies at Carlton House and his son's colossal debts, strained the royal relationship to the utmost. Then there was Burke's campaign to impeach Warren Hastings, who had returned to Britain in June 1785, for 'high crimes and misdemeanours' in India. And there was, as always, the national debt, more excise and higher taxes to complain about.

1
Wife and no wife, Gillray (1786) The marriage between the Prince of Wales and Mrs Fitzherbert violated both the Royal Marriage Act and the Act of Settlement. It was in fact performed in secret at Mrs Fitzherbert's home, but here Gillray imagines it in a French cathedral with Burke officiating (a reference to his championing of political concessions for RCs), Fox giving away the bride, and the driver North dozing till the ceremony is over.

2
The Political Banditti, Gillray (1786) A defence of Hastings against Burke's impeachment campaign. All armour-plated, Burke fires his ineffectual 'charges', North grabs as loot some honest revenue, while Fox prepares to stab Hastings in the back.

3
A Sale of English Beauties, Gillray (1786) A dandified auctioneer presides over the sale of a new consignment of courtesans to India. The indolence, luxury and excesses of some English communities in Madras were frequent talking-points in London. Publication of this print coincided with the departure of Cornwallis to India as the new Governor-General.

4
The Free-born Briton, Dent (1786) In March Pitt had appointed Commissioners for reducing the national debt through a sinking fund, and in his budget established a new excise scheme.

1

WIFE & no WIFE, or A trip to the Continent.

2

The POLITICAL BANDITTI assailing the SAVIOUR of INDIA.

A Sale of ENGLISH-BEAUTIES, in the EAST-INDIES.

THE FREE-BORN BRITON OR A PERSPECTIVE OF TAXATION.

1788–1789

THE REGENCY CRISIS

In October 1788 the King took to his bed with 'the flying gout' (as one of his doctors described the condition). Within a month it was clearly something else; the King was going to die. Over at Carlton House, Fox, the Prince of Wales and Mrs Fitzherbert prepared for their great moment. Pitt thought otherwise. The King was not yet dead —and if there was to be a regency it was going to be, like George II's, an ineffectual thing. By February 1789 he had introduced his Regency Bill depriving the Prince of Wales of any power to create peers or grant offices. But the King didn't die; on the 19th he began to recover and the crisis was over. Except for Fox and the Prince, who began to get some rough treatment from the mob whenever they showed their faces in the street.

1
Blood on Thunder fording the Red Sea, Gillray (1788) By the time Hastings' trial got under way in February 1788 much public opinion had swung against him, including Gillray's. Here Hastings and his loot are being carried across a sea of corpses by the Chancellor Thurlow, who presided over the trial but was openly against it.

2
A Peep behind the curtain at Drury Lane, Sayers (1788) Sheridan, an ardent Foxite, listens in dismay to the cries of the audience for the band to play 'God Save the King', at the height of the King's illness. Sheridan had campaigned furiously against a Regency Bill.

3
Filial Piety, Rowlandson (1788) The Prince of Wales is depicted bursting into his father's sickroom in a drunken frenzy, followed by his cronies (left is Sheridan). In fact, when the Prince was sent for the King attempted to strangle him.

4
Restoration Dressing Room, Kingsbury (1789) The King has recovered, against all expectation, and the ladies of Carlton House are having forlornly to join in the general thanksgiving with favours saying 'God save the King'. Even Mrs Fitzherbert (the Prince's feathers still on her head) is changing her garter.

80

1

BLOOD on THUNDER fording the RED SEA.

A Peep behind the Curtain at Drury Lane.

2

1790–1791

MONARCHY AND REPUBLICANISM

George III never entirely recovered from his derangement. More and more he withdrew from his public business and left Pitt to his own devices. When Pitt increased his Parliamentary majority in the general election of November 1790, his standing had never been higher. Nor, paradoxically, had the King's. This in some measure was due to public reaction to the excesses of the French Revolution (a reaction conditioned, more than anything, by the torrent of topical prints). They saw Louis XVI prevented (April 1791) from going to St Cloud by riots, a virtual prisoner in his own capital. They heard of his attempted escape in June, his capture at Varennes and return to Paris. They heard of massacres in the Champ de Mars, and were glad of a stable monarchy. In Birmingham rioters attacked the house of Joseph Priestley for his support of the Revolution. In London an irreconcilable quarrel broke out between Fox and Burke who had just published his Reflections on the Revolution in France.

1
Wierd Sisters, Gillray (1791) Dundas, the Home Secretary (left), Pitt and Thurlow anxiously search the sky for information about the King's future. The moon is made up of the face of George (in darkness) and Queen Charlotte who had assiduously guarded the King's interests and Pitt's during the Regency crisis. Speculations on the King's health of mind were legion at this time.

2
An Excrescence, Gillray (1791) Pitt is accused of usurping the prerogatives of the Crown during the King's withdrawal. His tentacles take on the shape of a crown.

3
The National Assembly Petrified, Gillray (1791) The news of Louis XVI's escape to Varennes reaches the Assembly.

4
The Knight of the Woeful Countenance, Anon (1790) A print ridiculing Burke's denunciation of the French Revolution. Burke is a biretta'd Don Quixote, his ass is the Pope and his shield is Aristocracy and Despotism.

5
Revolution Anniversary, Anon (1791) Priestley, Fox, Towers and Sheridan dance to celebrate the French Revolution around a witch's cauldron, which symbolizes the Anti-Levellers' headquarters (The Crown and Anchor Inn).

1

To H.Fuzelli Esq' this attempt in the Caricatura-Sublime, is respectfully dedicated

WIERD-SISTERS; MINISTERS of DARKNESS; MINIONS of the MOON
They should be Women! and yet their beards forbid us to interpret that they are so.

An Excrescence;—a Fungus;—alias—a Toadstool upon a Dunghill.
Pub. Dec. 20 1791 by H. Humphry N°. 18. old Bond street.

2

1792

QUEEN'S INFLUENCE

This year the Queen attracted the attention of the cartoonists. Pitt, it was alleged, had used her to restore his influence with the King after the failure in Parliament of his Russian Armament policy in 1791. To coerce the Empress Catherine to make peace with Turkey, Pitt had proposed to send a fleet to the Baltic. But for once the Opposition prevailed, through Fox in the Commons and Thurlow in the Lords. But in a direct confrontation between Pitt and Thurlow with the King, Thurlow was ousted (through the good offices, many believed, of Queen Charlotte). Not so well placed, however, was the French Queen, who found herself with the rest of the Royal Family in prison in August, as Austrian and Prussian troops advanced towards Paris. But after the Proclamation of the Republic in September, Britain watched with growing concern the successes of the French army as it crossed the Rhine and invaded the Austrian Netherlands.

1
Sin, Death and the Devil, Gillray (1792) The Queen (as Sin) intervenes in what would otherwise have been an unequal struggle between Pitt (Death) and Thurlow (the Devil). Cerberus, with the heads of his chief supporters, lies at Pitt's feet.

2
Anti-Saccharrites, Gillray (1792) A satire on the parsimony of the Royal household. There were that year protests against the slave trade in the form of a boycott against sugar. Queen Charlotte uses it as an excuse to get the Princesses to do without sugar at meals and so economize.

3
Design for the new Gallery of Busts and Pictures, Gillray (1792) For Fox's part in killing Pitt's Russian proposals, Empress Catherine had ordered a bust of Fox to be made.

1

ANTI-SACCHARRITES, – or – JOHN BULL and his Family leaving off the use of SUGAR.
To the Masters & Mistresses of Families in Great Britain, this Noble Example of ŒCONOMY, is respectfully submitted:

2

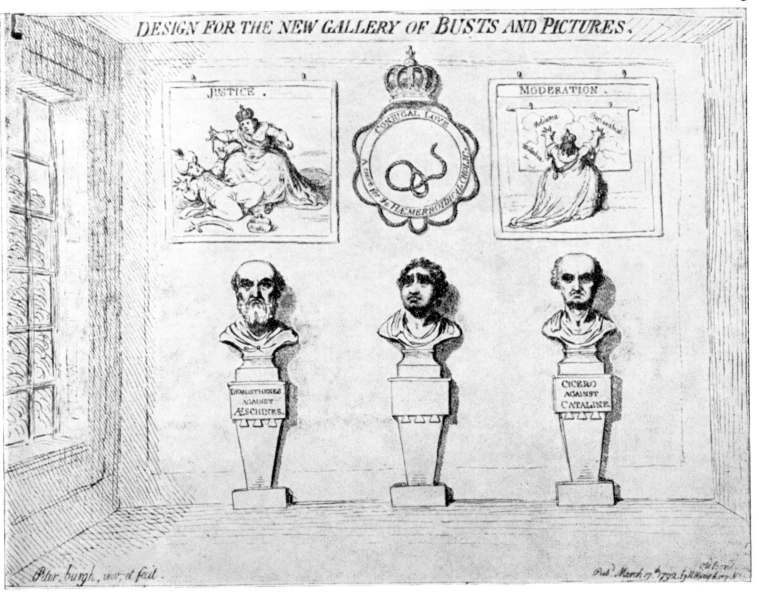

1793

THE REVOLUTIONARIES AT HOME

Anti-revolutionary satires focused largely on Priestley and Fox, and in particular Thomas Paine, whose *Rights of Man* had recently been published. In September 1792 he had fled to France and was later tried *in absentia* for publishing the book. To combat what was popularly believed to be an insidious English Jacobin takeover, an Anti-Leveller Society was formed. In the Commons the chief anti-leveller was Burke, whose dire warnings provided much grist to the mill of cartoonists' ridicule. In February 1793 the French themselves provided a more effective antidote by declaring war on Britain and Holland. Pitt responded promptly, issuing Exchequer Bills to raise defence funds and subsidies for Britain's allies (a coalition of new friends and ancient enemies—Spain, Holland, Prussia and Austria). At home the Traitorous Correspondence Act was passed and Habeas Corpus suspended. In Europe success in Corsica was quickly followed by defeat of the Duke of York in Holland.

1

Fashion before Ease, Gillray (1793) His face blotched with ink, Paine unceremoniously tries to fit Britannia's buxom form into French stays (of republicanism). A parody of Collett's painting of 1777.

2

Reflections on the French Revolution, I. Cruikshank (1793) A satire on Burke's campaign in the Commons against 'Republicans, Levellers, Regicides'. The violence of his attack alarms the Speaker and prompts Fox to exclaim 'Damme, he's got the French Disorder.'

3

Tom Paine's Nightly Pest, Gillray (1792) Paine dreams of the punishments that await him for his libels and crimes. At his head Fox and Priestley stand watch as his Guardian Angels.

4

The Chancellor of the Inquisition, Gillray (1793) Another dig at Burke's fanatical anti-leveller campaign. He makes out his Black List (which includes the Dukes of Norfolk and Portland) to deliver in the 'anonymous letter box' of the Crown and Anchor—the headquarters of the Anti-Leveller Society.

FASHION before EASE.

Reflections on the French Revolution.

The CHANCELLOR of the INQUISITION marking the INCORRIGIBLES

IV

PRIME MINISTERS AND THEIR PARTIES

1801–1804
Henry Addington (Tory)

1804–1806
William Pitt (Tory)

1806–1807
William Wyndham Grenville, Lord Grenville (Whig)

1807–1809
William Bentinck, Duke of Portland (Tory)

1809–1812
Spencer Perceval (Tory)

1812–1827
Robert Jenkinson, Earl of Liverpool (Tory)

CHAPTER IV

The Napoleonic Wars stirred the printshops to a crescendo of production and their artists to an unprecedented pitch of activity. But unlike the American war satires which had fuelled the fires of the colonists' cause, their successors remained for the most part loyal to the Administration (even if Pitt did have a few bad moments over food shortages and tax increases). During the early nineties the emphasis of the prints, many of them semi-official, was on the battles against republicanism in Britain, involving the machinations of the revolutionary societies and the vendettas of the counter-revolutionaries (notably the Anti-Levelling Society whose patronage of certain artists exposed it to the scorn of others).

Fox and his compatriots in the Whig Club bore the brunt of these attacks as their fortunes sunk lower and lower through the decade, hastened by their association with the Irish rebels, their French sympathies and their secession from the party following the rejection of Grey's motion for Reform in 1796.

George Cruikshank

The same year also saw the first appearance of Napoleon, in a Cruikshank production on the Italian Campaign. Yet in spite of the invasion panic of 1797, no wholehearted smear campaign was launched on him until the breakdown of the Peace of Amiens in 1803 stiffened British fibre; far from it, since many allusions up till then had been most flattering. But with Britain left isolated in Europe by the growth of Boney's Continental system and the political scene impoverished by the deaths of Pitt and Fox in the same year, he assumed his rightful position as Public Enemy Number One. All the weapons in the cartoonist's armoury were deployed against him—ridicule against the busy little gingerbread-maker, heavy irony against the upstart Corsican corporal, anger and indignation against the King of Terror. And at every step plucky little John Bull (sometimes, paradoxically representing the ailing King) stands in his path.

Gillray, whose onslaught on Napoleon had been continuous and memorable, produced his last political cartoon in 1810, after which he lapsed deeper and deeper into insanity until his death in 1815. His mantle fell on George Cruikshank (1792–1878) the son of Isaac and the brother of Robert, both cartoonists of some repute in their day. His first work had been on his father's plates, but after his death in 1811, George began publishing on his own account with immediate success. His Bonaparte caricatures were reproduced on pottery, and his contributions to William Hone's *Everyday Book* were powerful and influential social indictments, as well as a constant source of embarrassment to the Prince Regent. He later turned to book illustration (he drew the original illustrations for *Oliver Twist*) and to temperance reform—a cause in which he was rather less successful. The tragically short career of Robert Newton (1778–98) is also of this period. In his brief twenty-one years this gifted caricaturist appears to have had a distinguished, if dangerous, career, publishing his first work in his early teens, acquiring a fashionable circle of admirers and being thrown into jail during the sedition-hunts of 1793–94.

1794–1795
RUMOURS OF INVASION

In Paris the Terror reached its height. News arrived in Britain of the execution of Marie Antoinette at the end of 1793, later of Danton and Robespierre. Radical associations in Britain continued, however, to demand Parliamentary reform. In July 1794 the Whigs were split on the issue, Portland and Wyndham joining Pitt's Cabinet, Fox and Grey leading a rump of forty. But the progress of the war held out little comfort to Pitt either; the French armies overran Spain in 1794 and Holland in 1795 making an invasion of Britain a very real threat. Public outcry against heavy taxation and rocketing food prices reached a peak in the summer: Pitt's house was mobbed and in October the King, driving to open Parliament, was attacked in his coach. To forestall mob rule Pitt had within a month introduced his Treasonable Practices Bill and a Seditious Meetings Bill, which forbade gatherings of more than fifty persons to be held without notice to a magistrate.

1
French Invasion or Brighton in a Bustle, Nixon (1794) As French military successes increased, so did fears at home of an invasion. The volunteers though, who would have to bear the brunt, became a public joke. Here they are made up of chambermaids, farm-hands and even the bathing-ladies of the Brighton beaches.

2
Patriotic Regeneration, Gillray (1794) The imaginary results of French conquest: Parliament is remodelled on French lines. The Opposition and the radical associations are united in impeaching Pitt. Fox is the presiding judge, Sheridan his clerk of the court. Stanhope, as Public Prosecutor, reads the charge against Pitt, the first of which is 'For opposing the right of subjects to dethrone the King'.

3
The Royal Extinguisher, I. Cruikshank (1795) Pitt as a watchman uses his extinguisher (which rapidly became a symbol in cartoons for law and order) to put down a seditious meeting of Fox, Sheridan and their supporters, who have gathered at Copenhagen (House).

1

FRENCH INVASION OR BRIGHTON IN A BUSTLE.

Patriotic Regeneration ___ viz. ___ Parliament Reform'd a la Françoise ___ that is ___ Honest Men (i.e. Opposition) in the Seat of Justice

The ROYAL EXTINGUISHER or GULLIVER Putting out the PATRIOTS of LILLIPUT!!!

Two of Gillray's more ambitious Pittite productions, both celebrating his supposed rescue of the Constitution from the hands of revolutionaries and levellers.

1
Light expelling Darkness, Gillray (1795) Attended by Justice and driving a team of the British Lion and the Horse of Hanover, Pitt puts to flight the Whig Club (bottom left), the revolutionary conspirators Sheridan, Fox and Stanhope (bottom right) and countless Jacobins. The allegory is too overblown for it not to be ironic.

2
The Death of the Great Wolf, Gillray (1795) In this parody of Benjamin West's *Death of Wolfe*, Pitt (supported by Burke, Arden and Dundas) expires at his moment of triumph. The Opposition has been routed by his Convention Bill.

1

94

The DEATH of the Great WOLF.

1796–1797

PITT RESTORED

After the buffetings of the previous year Pitt's political stature improved. In March he began peace negotiations with France through the Swiss Minister, but Napoleon's Italian Campaign was proving a great success, and by the end of the year Spain had declared war, the Royal Navy had withdrawn from the Mediterranean and the impudent French attempted, unsuccessfully, to land at Bantry Bay. 1797 found him in full battle-cry, drumming up money through Loyalty loans, tripling assessed taxes, overriding naval mutinies at the Nore and Spithead and finally forcing Fox, in his despair, to go into voluntary retirement from politics. One of his few reversals was the defeat of Wilberforce's bill for abolition of the slave trade (April 1796), in support of which he had spoken passionately.

1
Philanthropic Consolations, Gillray (1796) After the narrow defeat of their Slave Bill, Wilberforce and the Bishop of Rochester are depicted drowning their sorrows in the company of two voluptuous negresses. A print possibly commissioned by the West India block.

2
The Giant Factotum amusing himself, Gillray (1797) A reflection of Pitt's restored influence. Straddling the Speaker's chair and using a globe for the fashionable game of Cup and Ball, his right foot is kissed and venerated by Tories (including Wilberforce and Dundas), his left foot crushes the Opposition of Erskine, Sheridan, Grey and Fox.

3
William the Conqueror's triumphal entry, Newton (1796) Led by a gloating Dundas, Pitt rides (John) Bull and his burden of Loyalty Loans into the Treasury.

4
The Orangerie, Gillray (1797) William V of Orange had fled from the invading French army in 1795 and taken up residence at Hampton Court. His indolence, his lack of support for the Duke of York's forces and his success with serving-girls were all the subject of common gossip.

The GIANT-FACTOTUM amusing himself.

WILLIAM THE CONQUEROR'S TRIUMPHAL ENTRY!!!

The ORANGERIE; or — the Dutch Cupid reposing, after the fatigues of Planting. — Vide The Visions in Hampton Bower.

1797–1799

PITT ON THE WARPATH

Invasion panic redoubled when it was heard that Napoleon had been put in command of forces to attack Britain. When the French fleet left Toulon for Egypt, it was widely believed to be heading for Ireland, where a rebellion had broken out. The inadequacy of national defences forced Pitt to even sterner tax measures; the hated Assessment Tax gave way to the even more loathed Income Tax (of all incomes over £200). In August 1798 Nelson destroyed the French fleet at the Battle of the Nile. In October a genuine French invasion of Ireland collapsed. The Egyptian victory and the confession of the Irish rebel O'Connor that he had had a hand in the invasion discomfited the Whigs even further and brought Foxite fortunes to their lowest level. Despite the capitulation of the Duke of York's army in Holland, the century closed with Pitt having secured strong alliances in Europe (the Second Coalition) and having much to look forward to.

1
St George's Volunteers, Gillray (1797) No amount of invasion fever could transform the volunteers from figures of fun into a serious component of national defence.

2
A Visitor to John Bull for the year 1799, Anon (1798) Another contribution in the time-honoured tradition of anti-tax propaganda; this time criticizing Pitt's wartime Income Tax.

3
John Bull taking a Luncheon, Gillray (1798) In celebration of Nelson's victory on the Nile, John Bull makes a meal of enemy ships served up by Nelson, Howe (defeated the French fleet in the Channel 1794), Duncan (victor at Camperdown against the Dutch 1797), Warren (who prevented the French invasion of Ireland), Gardiner, Hood and Jervis. Outside the window Fox and Sheridan make off in dismay at the frustration of all their expectations.

4
Stealing off, Gillray (1798) Confronted with the evidence ('End of the Irish rebellion', 'Capture of the French navy', 'Europe arming'), Fox escapes from the House, while his supporters eat their words.

2

JOHN BULL taking a Luncheon:— or —British Cooks, cramming Old Grumble-Gizzard with Bonne Chere.

Stealing off;— or — prudent Secesion:—

1800–1802

A PRECARIOUS PEACE

On January 1st, 1801, Pitt's efforts to form a political union between England and Ireland were rewarded with the Act of Union, by which the first joint Parliament came into force. Not so happily omened was his advocacy of Catholic Emancipation, first proposed in September 1800, but which brought about his resignation in March of the following year. His ministry was succeeded by Addington's, mediocre in comparison, but granted an auspicious beginning with a striking victory by Nelson over the Danish fleet at Copenhagen. The Armed Neutrality (of Russia, Sweden, Denmark and Prussia) which had bedevilled British shipping for months broke up in June, and peace negotiations going on all through the summer looked like bearing fruit. In October the peace preliminaries were signed by which Britain agreed to part, among many of her maritime conquests, with Malta.

1
The Union Club, Gillray (1800) The scene is the first meeting of the new Union Club, a gathering of Whigs presided over by the Prince of Wales (who has fallen under the table). The Opposition resented the new arrangements for Ireland and are here drowning their sorrows, among them the inevitable Sheridan and Fox (left).

2
The Cow-Pock, Gillray (1802) In this year Jenner was awarded a Parliamentary grant for his researches into inoculation, and had opened a clinic in St Pancras.

3
The Balance of Power, Williams (1802) Napoleon, whose ten-year term as First Consul had begun in 1800, was still commanding some respect in Britain. Heavily outweighed by him, Pitt and Addington exclaim: 'So this is the balance of power we have been making such a fuss about—a pretty piece of business we have made of it.'

4
The first Kiss this Ten Years!, Gillray (1803) The Peace of Amiens was signed in March 1802, but in this reconciliation scene between France and Britain, Britannia looks justifiably apprehensive, for Napoleon had continued his conquests, first in Piedmont, then in Elba and Switzerland.

2

1803–1804

FROM PEACE BACK TO WAR
The Peace lasted barely fourteen months. Napoleon continued to meddle in Swiss and Italian affairs; Britain refused to part with Malta without guarantees that were not forthcoming. In May an embargo was placed on all French and Dutch ships in British ports. France responded by completing her occupation of Hanover and inspiring yet another rebellion in Ireland. Addington's inability to cope with a war situation was manifest, but removing him turned out to be a tricky job. Grenville and Windham refused to take office without Fox, but, at the King's insistence, he found himself excluded when Pitt finally ousted Addington over the Irish Militia Bill in April 1804. The same week Napoleon was proclaimed Emperor and crowned in December by Pope Pius VII.

1
A Phantasmagoria, Gillray (1803)   The three witches (left to right : Addington, Fox and Hawkesbury) stew up the remains of the British Lion and fuel the fire with Britain's lost assets, Malta, Dominion of the Seas, Continental alliances, etc. In the foreground Wilberforce (a vehement peace advocate) incants over the proceedings in unison with a French cock.

2
A Stoppage to a Stride over the Globe, Roberts (1803)   Napoleon's progress across Europe had been in direct violation of the Peace of Amiens. 'Little Johnny Bull' bravely opposes his designs against Britain (or it could be— the artist's geography is purely symbolic—Malta).

3
The Save-all and the Extinguisher, Anon (1803)   The King's popularity in Britain increased as Napoleon's diminished. He wields the repeated symbol of British law and order (a watchman's extinguisher) to snuff out the puny Corsican flame.

4
Britannia between Death and the Doctors, Gillray (1804)   Dr Pitt with his bottle of 'Constitutional Restorative' ousts the old ministry of Dr Addington with his 'Composing Draft'. Fox's hopes of office are dashed in the fracas. Behind the curtain, a reminder that Napoleon (as Death) still lies in wait for the ailing Britannia.

102

A PHANTASMAGORIA ;— Scene Conjuring up an Armed Skeleton.

A STOPPAGE to a STRIDE over the GLOBE

The Save-all and the Extinguisher!!

1805–1806
THE DEATHS OF PITT AND FOX

In 1805 the declaration of war against Britain by Spain was partially countered by Pitt's success in forming yet another coalition against France. Rejoicing at Nelson's victory at Trafalgar was tempered by news of Napoleon's rout of the Russians and Austrians at Austerlitz. But the undiluted disaster for the Pittites was the death of Pitt himself in January 1806. The inheritors of the war became Grenville's administration (the Ministry of all the Talents, as it was ironically dubbed), with Fox as Foreign Secretary, and all Pittites excluded. It made an inauspicious start: its peace negotiations were widely despised, its tax impositions (the increase of Income Tax with a lower exemption limit) universally execrated. And then in September Fox died. In an effort for Grenville (whose long-standing reputation was that of a sinecurist) to attract more supporters through patronage, Parliament was dissolved. In the ensuing election he was swept back with a great majority though Sheridan, who had assumed Fox's mantle, had only the narrowest of victories in his constituency.

1

The Plumb-pudding in danger, Gillray (1805) One of Gillray's most famous plates shows Pitt and Napoleon dividing up a world ('too small to satisfy such insatiable appetites') between them. Napoleon's unofficial peace overtures in a letter to George III in January were sceptically received and replied to with calls to 'prosecute the war with vigour'.

2

Tiddy Doll, Gillray (1806) With Napoleon's hegemony in Europe confirmed after Austerlitz he (in the guise of a famous, fast-talking Mayfair gingerbread-maker) prepares to plant assorted friends and relatives on vacant thrones—Joseph for Naples, Louis for Holland, Jerome for Westphalia, Talleyrand for Benevento, etc. The 'next batch of viceroys' on the chest includes members of the Opposition.

3

Visiting the Sick, Gillray (1806) A vicious satire on Fox's fatal illness in June. Around him stand Mrs Fitzherbert as an Abbess ('Do confess your sins, Charley'), the bishop of Meath ('If you're spared this time give us emancipation'), the Prince of Wales, Sheridan, Grey and others.

1

TIDDY-DOLL the great French Gingerbread-Baker, drawing out a new Batch of Kings.

2

VISITING the SICK.

1805–1806

THE MINISTRY OF ALL THE TALENTS

1
Falstaff and his Followers vindicating the Property Tax, Rowlandson (1806) One of the first acts of the new ministry had been to raise the hated Income Tax.

2
Charley's old Breeches in Danger, Gillray (1807) Grenville's Ministry of all the Talents (otherwise known as the Broad-bottomed Ministry) gorge themselves on the fruits of office in a pair of Fox's old trousers. On the left Pittites, Castlereagh, Canning, Perceval and Rose try to pull them down. On the right Radicals, Cobbett, Burdett and Horne Took attempt to lever them off, using as fulcrum the Scottish tailor Paull, who almost succeeded in defeating Sheridan in the election.

3
The Friend of the People, Gillray (1806) A satire on the taxes presented to the people in Fox's budget, including the levy on private breweries (see right).

2

The FRIEND of the PEOPLE," & his Petty New-Tax-Gatherer, paying John Bull a visit!

1807–1809
BRITAIN ALONE AGAINST EUROPE

Profoundly unpopular, Grenville's ministry lasted barely three months into 1807. It came unstuck over the question of Catholic Emancipation, to which the King was irrevocably opposed. In March the Whigs surrendered their seals of office, never to emerge again in George III's reign. In May a general election was held on the issue of 'No Popery' and although Portland's ministry was returned (with Canning and Castlereagh) it was notable more for the support given to the Radicals with their platform for Parliamentary Reform. Domestic matters, however, were overshadowed by the Treaty of Tilset between Napoleon and the Tsar which aimed at, and effected, the complete isolation of Britain. The Bourbon rising against Napoleon's brother Joseph in June, however, once again gave Britain the toe-hold she needed in Europe. Wellesley's triumphs in the Peninsula in 1809 did much to relieve the gloom at home.

1
The Genius of the Election, Woodward (1807) The results of the 'No Popery' election did little to enhance the standing of any political faction, with the exception of the Radicals.

2
The Valley of the Shadow of Death, Gillray (1808) Down a path between Styx (where King Joseph is sinking) and Lethe (where the reptiles Holland, America, etc, are floundering) Napoleon leads his Russian Bear tamed by the treaty of Tilset. Advancing against him are the British Lion, Death on a Spanish charger and the Portuguese Wolf. Even the Pope (whose Papal states were annexed in May) descends on him like a meteor.

3
The Head of the Family in Good Humour, Woodward and Rowlandson (1809) Undisturbed John Bull is surrounded by the enmity of (from left) Napoleon, Russia, Holland, America (whose Non-intercourse Act refused trade with Britain and France in reprisal at their restrictions), Prussia, Austria, Spain (reoccupied by Napoleon at end of 1808) and Denmark.

1

THE GENIUS OF ELECTION or John Bulls Resolution

2

THE VALLEY OF THE SHADOW OF DEATH.

1810–1812

NAPOLEON IN RETREAT

1810 found the Government in disarray: the previous year Portland had given way to Perceval because of ill-health, and Canning fought a duel with Castlereagh over incompetence in the War Office. Now the King's health was failing, a Regency seemed imminent and the Opposition's hopes were high. There was trouble with the Radicals: Cobbett had to be put away for seditious libel in his *Register* and there were riots in Piccadilly over Burdett's committal to the Tower for breach of privilege. And Napoleon was doing his best to prevent the import (or smuggling) of British goods into Europe. The tide of war didn't change until 1811, with a trickle of good news from Portugal, where the Duke of Wellington's campaign was prospering, and from Russia where the Tsar was reported to have been alienated from Napoleon. By the autumn of 1812 it had turned into a flood—Wellington had entered Madrid, Napoleon was being forced to retreat from Moscow. At home two events—the establishment of an unrestricted Regency in February and the assassination of Perceval in May—caused a flurry of political lobbying and speculation, the outcome of which (to the Whigs' bitterest disappointment with their erstwhile ally, the Prince of Wales) was an administration under Lord Liverpool.

1
The Borough Mongers strangled in the Tower, Rowlandson (1810) After his imprisonment in the Tower, Burdett gained the stature—in the popular imagination—of a latter-day Wilkes, a champion of liberty and parliamentary reform.

2
The Valley of the Shadow of Death, Elmes (1812) The circumstances of Gillray's print of the same name (see above) are reversed. Now the Russian Bear turns on Napoleon and out of the flames of the Kremlin Palace come the Muscovy Cat, the Dagger of Revenge and the Russian Scourge.

3
Boney Hatching a Bulletin, G. Cruikshank (1812) The extent of the Russian disaster dawned on the British public in December as the later bulletins reached London.

THE BOROUGH MONGERS STRANGLED IN THE TOWER.

THE VALLEY OF THE SHADOW OF DEATH.

2

Boney Hatching a Bulletin or Snug Winter Quarters!!!

1813-1814

ALLIES TRIUMPHANT

In 1813 the country contrived to get itself involved in war on two fronts. The long history of trade squabbles and shipping violations with the United States had erupted into open war in June the previous year. By the autumn of 1813 Britain had been forced to abandon whole stretches of the Canadian frontier. In Europe, however, first Prussia then Austria declared war on Napoleon, Wellington entered France and at the 'Battle of the Nations' at Leipzig in October the French were decisively beaten. Even then Napoleon was evasive about the terms of the Frankfurt peace proposals, compelling the allies to invade France. 1814 was a year of profound relief for Britain: in March Paris was occupied and at the Treaty of Fontainebleau Napoleon abdicated unconditionally and was banished to Elba. In August a British force reached Washington and burnt it; in December the Treaty of Ghent ended the American war as well.

1
The Yankee Torpedo, Elmes (1813) One of the features of the American War had been the use of Fulton's torpedo to break the New York blockade.

2
The Two Kings of Terror, Rowlandson (1813) A celebration of Napoleon's defeat at Leipzig.

3
Broken Gingerbread, G. Cruikshank (1814) Turning up in guise of Tiddy Doll ('Removed from Paris'), a tattered Napoleon attempts to hawk his 'images of Emperor and Kings' for export, from Elba.

1

2

BROKEN GINGERBREAD

1814–1815
THE PRICE OF VICTORY

With news of Napoleon's fall the celebrations in London were lavish and, with food prices dropping and trade beginning to circulate again, public humour was restored. In November 1814 the Congress of Vienna opened, but was soon splitting itself into factions, secret alliances and vested interests. In March of the next year their deliberations were rudely interrupted by Napoleon's return to Paris for the beginning of his 'Hundred Days', but the map of Europe had been redrawn by the time of Wellington and Blucher's victory at Waterloo and Napoleon's positively final abdication. At home there were murmurings in the City about the proposed Corn Bill, forbidding the import of cheap French corn when the average price at home was below 80 shillings a quarter. Parliamentary opposition and petitions to the Regent failed to halt its passage.

1
Peace and Plenty, G. Cruikshank (1814) A jolly print of John Bull dining with Louis XVIII on all the goodies that peace (and the courtesy of the Prince Regent, top right) had made available—bread at 9d a loaf, beer at 3d a tankard etc.

2
The European Pantomime, Marks (1815) Napoleon's return from Elba (as Harlequin) to depose Louis XVIII (as Pantaloon) is blamed on the posturings and folly of the assembled nations at the Congress of Vienna.

3
The Genius of France, G. Cruikshank (1815) A satire attacking Napoleon's reception in Paris in March.

4
The Blessings of Peace, G. Cruikshank (1815) An implication that the Corn Bill was an attempt to protect the interests of landowners by keeping the price of corn artificially high, thereby starving the honest workman and his family.

1

PEACE & PLENTY or good news for JOHN BULL!!!

The European Pantomime

2

3

4

CHAPTER

PRIME MINISTERS AND THEIR PARTIES

1812–1827
Robert Jenkinson, Earl of Liverpool (Tory)

1827
George Canning (Tory)

1827–1828
Frederick Robinson, Viscount Goderich (Tory)

1828–1830
Arthur Wellesley, Duke of Wellington (Tory)

1830–1834
Charles Grey, Earl Grey (Whig)

1834
William Lamb, Viscount Melbourne (Whig)

1834–1835
Sir Robert Peel (Tory)

1834–1841
William Lamb, Viscount Melbourne (Whig)

1841–1846
Sir Robert Peel (Tory)

1846–1852
John Russell, Earl Russell (Whig)

117

CHAPTER V

With the end of a quarter of a century's nearly continuous war came the end of the England of the eighteenth century. The population was slowly draining from its enclosed countryside to the industrial districts, a new breed of manufacturer was emerging to challenge the status of the landowners (who still held firmly on to the reins of government). Johnson's England was giving way to Cobbett's.

Peace did not bring plenty, not for the mass of Englishmen whose corporate voice began to be heard, not as aimless mob-enthusiasm for any cause a rabble-rouser cared to invoke but as a positive political force under the direction of men like Owen, O'Connor and Cobden. It was no accident that the overwhelming majority of cartoons of this period are domestic. Beneath the gracious life-style and exquisite taste of post-Regency society there runs the accelerating undercurrent of popular agitation for reform and the embryo of working-class unity, which was to have irresistible repercussions on the cartoonists themselves.

In the 1820s came the end of the boom for the print-sellers. They had been established for a hundred years and had prospered exceedingly for fifty of them. But the demand for etchings in the Gillray tradition began to die out: as an art-form it had long reached its peak and the quality of inventiveness and execution was not being maintained. After 1821 Cruikshank himself abandoned political caricature, leaving the field to the prolific William Heath (1795–1840), who must be considered the last of the old school. His robust and pleasing style found its most pertinent targets in the opening acts of the drama of the First Reform Bill. But by the time the Bill had become a reality he, too, had vanished.

His place was taken by Robert Seymour (1800–36), who took over his position as caricaturist for *The Looking Glass*, a monthly broadsheet of political cartoons, and by John Doyle (1797–1868), whose kindly lithographs were extravagantly rated second only to Gillray's in his lifetime. It was not that politics lacked the passion of earlier generations, for the Reform Bill, the Free Trade controversy, Chartism and many other domestic issues were all of the stuff that vitriolic cartoons are made of; it was simply a reflection of the rather more gentlemanly way politics were conducted, in public if not in fact. John Doyle particularly (drawing under the pseudonym of 'H.B.') set the style of percipient commentary, as opposed to offensive propaganda, that was later to be the hallmark of Victorian cartoons.

There were, in the thirties and forties, exceptions to this new tradition in the underground broadsheets which circulated among the many militant associations and movements for industrial and franchise reform. Cheap, often crude but undeniably virile, these publications disregarded such niceties as the stamp tax and were therefore illegal, yet they flourished and produced a number of artists (notably C. J. Grant) whose wood-engravings recalled some of the fervour of the eighteenth-century nameless cartoonists.

The mortal blow to the individually published print came with the marriage between graphic satire and journalism. Caricature magazines had existed, with varying life-spans, in the early nineteenth century: the *Scourge, The Satirist*, the *Monthly Meteor, The Looking Glass, Figaro*. But none proved to be more in tune with the developing Victorian middle-class culture than *Punch*, whose first issue appeared in July 1841. Its advent was quickly followed by that of *The Illustrated London News* (May 1842), but where the *ILN* employed its artists as observers, *Punch* though equally decorous employed them as commentators. Its hegemony in the world of cartoons, if not always for the best, was absolute for virtually all of Victoria's reign.

Punch's first leading political cartoonist was John Leech (1817–64), whose description of the frescoes to decorate the new Houses of Parliament gave us the word 'cartoon' in its modern sense. Leech's output for *Punch* was enormous and it earned him a great deal of money, but in retrospect it is his social satires which linger in the memory, for they were genuinely funny where his political efforts often lacked an edge. Richard Doyle's (1824–83) work, though largely overshadowed by Leech's at the time, probably seems more effective to modern eyes. He was the son of 'H.B.' and learnt his art from his father, but his promising career was cut short by an irreconcilable quarrel with *Punch* over the magazine's dedicated anti-Catholic policy.

1816–1817

RIOTS AND REPRESSION

Two years of unrest followed the ending of the war. There was much to complain about: Income Tax which many thought would be abolished—but was not; a slump in trade which caused widespread hardships; a standing army to pay for and royal extravagance, including two marriages and the Regent's taste for the exotic. Violence erupted in December 1816 at Spa Fields when a crowd, assembled to hear demands for political reform, marched on London. In January the Prince Regent's coach was fired on as he returned from the Opening of Parliament. When a secret Parliamentary committee reported that an insurrection was imminent, the Government acted promptly and repressively. Habeas Corpus was suspended, Acts for the Protection of the King and Regent and for the Prevention of Seditious Meetings were passed, and all magistrates received a circular advising them to suppress seditious publications. Predictably the public response was violent: the 'March of the Blanketeers' set off from Manchester to London and was turned back at Stockport; in Derbyshire there were riots against low wages and unemployment.

1

The British Atlas, Williams (1816) The war is over, but John Bull stoically continues to support the burden of a standing army (which in turn is propping up Louis XVIII). Napoleon stands like a Colossus on St Helena in the distance.

2

A Swarm of English Bees, G. Cruikshank (1816) One of the great attractions of the year was an exhibition of Napoleon's relics, particularly his coach captured at Waterloo.

3

A Peep into the Green Bag, Marks (1817) The gullibility of Parliament's secret committee to examine evidence of sedition was much ridiculed. Here they examine the strangest assortment of 'evidence' through magnifying glasses and come to absurd conclusions.

4

A Poet Mounted, Williams (1817) A great disappointment to the Radicals was Southey's 'defection' from the Republican cause by accepting the job of Poet Laureate.

THE BRITISH ATLAS, or John Bull supporting the Peace Establishment

A Peep in to the GREEN BAG or the Secret Committee of MAGNIFIERS.

A POET MOUNTED on the COURT PEGASUS.

1818–1819

AFTERMATH OF PETERLOO

Economic conditions improved slowly, but agitation continued over Parliamentary reform and the Corn Laws. An attempt to repeal the Septennial Act was defeated in May, as was (overwhelmingly) Burdett's motion for annual parliaments and universal suffrage. In August 1819 a crowd that had gathered in St Peter's Fields, Manchester, to press for reform and repeal of the Corn Laws was charged by the Militia, and many were killed. After the 'Peterloo Massacre' the Government was reduced to even more authoritarian measures than it had adopted two years earlier. The infamous Six Acts provided for wider powers for magistrates to search for arms, higher penalties for seditious libel, a harder clampdown on public meetings and the introduction of stamp duty on newspapers (which had achieved an unprecedented level of viciousness and scurrility).

1
The Dandy Club, Dighton (1818) Heir to the Beaus and the Macaronis of the eighteenth century were the Dandies, whose fashions dominated the Regency period.

2
Poor Bull and his Burden, G. Cruikshank (1819) Cartoonists continued to inveigh against the level of taxation, but it is no longer the King of France John Bull is supporting but the whole hierarchy of power and privilege from landed gentry to monarchy.

3
Massacre at St Peters, Cruikshank, (1819) The Militia epitomize corrupt and landed interests: the captain urges them on with the reminder that 'the more you kill the less poor rates you have to pay'. An eyewitness of the Peterloo Massacre records 'Women, white-vested maids and tender youths were indiscriminately sabred or trampled' (Samuel Bedford).

4
A Free Born Englishman, Anon (1819) Unable to pay his taxes Mr Bull has been removed to the debtor's prison and is now deprived of his basic right to protest by the imposition of the Six Acts.

5
The Ladies' Accelerator, R. Cruikshank (1819) Velocipedes were the innovation of the year (even banned in London as a danger to horse traffic).

The DANDY CLUB.

Poor BULL & his Burden — or the Political MURRAIN !!!
"And the land stank — so num'rous was the fry."
— What will become of these Vermin, if the Bull should Rise—? !!!!!!!!!!!

Massacre at St Peters or "BRITONS STRIKE HOME"!!!

A FREE BORN ENGLISHMAN!
THE ADMIRATION of the WORLD!!!
AND THE ENVY of SURROUNDING NATIONS!!!!!

123

1820–1826

THE CAROLINE AFFAIR

For the first half of George IV's reign there was little at home or abroad to stir up the cartoonists to their earlier frenzies. There were passing sensations like the discovery of the Cato Street conspiracy to murder Cabinet ministers in 1820 and Castlereagh's suicide in 1822. There was a prestigious foreign policy under Canning, there was reform, of prisons by Peel and of child labour in mills and factories, and there was always the sinister undertow of pressure for Catholic Emancipation. But to a large degree the prints were preoccupied with fashions, taste and above all the King. His affair with Lady Conyngham and the Caroline Affair (1820–21) stimulated them to shades of their former nastiness. In June 1820 the Princess of Wales triumphantly returned to London from her self-imposed exile, demanding her rightful recognition as Queen. The King, who had long wished to divorce her, prompted Parliament to introduce the Bill of Pains and Penalties (to deprive her of titles and dissolve the marriage). Such was the popular (and Radical) support for Caroline, and so discredited was the evidence brought forward at the enquiry into her conduct abroad, that the Bill was dropped like a hot brick, Parliament prorogued, the Queen granted an annuity of £50,000 and the King put into bad odour for a long time to come.

1
Coronation, G. Cruikshank (1820)
Hone's political pamphlets (from which this is taken) were a constant source of embarrassment to the King during the Caroline affair. Instead of a crown, a green bag (traditional symbol of secret official inquiries) is being deposited on his head.

2
Reflection, R. Cruikshank (1821)
George IV, trying on the crown for size of Caroline in his looking-glass, already wearing the crown to which she was laying claim.

3
A King-Fisher, Williams (1826)
Windsor, where he had reconstructed the castle on a monumental scale, was the King's regular bolthole at times of crisis and Lady Conyngham (like others of his mistresses, a grandmother) his constant companion.

1

" Le Roy le veut!" G. R.

See Blackstone's Com. b. 1. c. 2.

REFLECTION

2

A KING-FISHER.

4

Mer de Glace, Anon (1821) The Napoleonic Wars had cut the English cognoscenti off from their Grand Tours of France and Italy. But with the coming of peace and the opening up of Europe once more the English resumed their role of intrepid tourists in increasing numbers—and in much more adventurous places.

5

Nashional Taste!!! G. Cruikshank (1824) The name of Thomas Nash has become synonymous with the best in Regency architecture, but by no means all his constructions were kindly received at the time (as for instance his All Souls, Langham Place which was heavily criticized in Parliament and the Press, and on which he is here spiked).

6

Corinthian Steamers, Heath (1825) Smoking had been brought back into fashion by the Dandies (and the veterans of the Peninsular War), but indulging in the habit out of doors or in the presence of ladies was still frowned upon.

7

The Political Toy-man, R. Cruikshank (1825) The urge towards self-education (or The March of Intellect as the cartoonists ridiculed it) was a notable trend of the reign, which saw George Birkbeck found the Mechanics' Institute and the opening of University and King's College London. Henry Brougham (cartooned here) was a prime mover behind University College—which was denounced by some as a political manoeuvre—and the founder of the Society for the Diffusion of Useful Knowledge.

8

Beauties of Brighton, Crowquill and Cruikshank (1826) The King's extravaganza at Brighton, The Royal Pavillion (completed 1820), is the background for this fashionable setpiece which includes Tallyrand (right) and the artist (left, centre of the three dandies).

Mer de Glace —— Sea of Ice.

NASHIONAL TASTE !!!
(Dedicated, without permission, to the Church Commissioners)

CORINTHIAN STEAMERS *or Costumes and Customs of 1824* London Pub Feb 26 1824 by SW Fores 41 Picadilly

The POLITICAL TOY-MAN.

Beauties of BRIGHTON

1827–1829

CATHOLIC RELIEF AND LAW AND ORDER

In less than twelve months the country witnessed the comings and goings of four prime ministers. In February 1827 Liverpool suffered a stroke and gave way to Canning's ministry of liberal Tories and moderate Whigs. Canning's death in August was followed by Goderich's ineffectual leadership. In January 1828 the Duke of Wellington assembled an exclusively Tory administration, whose first significant success was the repeal of the Test and Corporation Acts (by which Catholics and Nonconformists were now eligible for public office) and which paved the way for complete Catholic Emancipation the next year. With the passing of the Roman Catholic Relief Bill in April 1829 Catholics were further given the right of suffrage, and to sit and vote in Parliament. All this in the teeth of adamant opposition from the King, whose obsession with extravagant building and exotic tastes was also currently evoking howls of protest from the cartoonists (the more so since 1829 was promising a bad harvest and industrial distress). Abroad, Britain dabbled diplomatically in the Eastern Question (Greece's struggle for independence and the Russo-Turkish War). At home, Peel turned to law and order reform, reducing the number of capital offences in 1827 and founding the London police force in 1829.

1
A Kick up among the Whigs, Heath (1828) Little w(h)igs are sent headlong by the arrival of Wellington's Tory ministry. He was constantly satirized as a militaristic premier and criticized for maintaining his influence in the army. It was a job for which, he himself had said, 'he was not qualified'.

2
Portrait of a Noble Duke, Anon (1829) Wellington's head is made up, in 'emblematic' style, of the accoutrements of war—reminiscent of a famous portrait of Napoleon in 1814.

3
Mrs Greece and her Rough Lovers, Seymour (1828) In 1827 Turkey had occupied Athens and rejected an Anglo-Franco-Russian demand for a truce with Greece. In April 1828 Russia declared war on Turkey. John Bull looks on in some concern that 'Old Nick will have her' (i.e. that the Tsar would solve the Eastern Question without reference to his allies).

4
Searching an English Ship in the Dardanelles, Heath (1829) Russian aggression in the Eastern Mediterranean extended even to the boarding and searching of her allies' ships.

128

1

A KICK UP AMONG THE WIGS.

PORTRAIT OF A NOBLE DUKE.

I should think this head possest some talent for Military affairs.
Wellington

2

Mr GREECE and HER ROUGH LOVERS

Searching an English Ship in the DARDANELLES — or our faithful Ally showing his respect for the British Flag

129

4

5

Peeling a Charley, Heath (1829) The last watchmen (Charlies) disappeared from the London streets on Michaelmas Day when 1000 of Robert Peel's new Police Force took over. The watchmen had been derided as incompetents; the new police were criticized as authoritarian.

6

Finis, Heath (1829) While Peel kneels to receive the King's signature on the Catholic Relief Bill, the Chancellor's mace obscures the Coronation Oath and Wellington covers up George III's (doubtless) agonized expression. George III had absolutely refused to countenance emancipation for Catholics, believing religiously in the inviolable nature of his Coronation Oath, which if he denied he would forfeit the Crown.

7

State of the Nation, Seymour (1829) This year saw a crisis of overproduction with its attendant hardships for the working-man.

8

The Great Joss and his Playthings, Seymour (1829) On George IV's passion for *chinoiserie* and his ambitious building projects. A model of the Brighton Pavilion is behind him, models of Buckingham Palace and Hyde Park Gate in front of him. The shelf is crammed with unfinished churches.

5

6

STATE OF THE NATION

THE GREAT JOSS AND HIS PLAYTHINGS.

1828–1830

VISIONS OF THE INDUSTRIAL REVOLUTION

The urban revolution which had been incubating around them had been largely ignored by the cartoonists—until the end of the '20s. Since peace had come to Britain after the Napoleonic Wars, there had been a remarkable leap forward in the technological applications of scientific discovery, in methods of production and means of communication. MacAdam's method of road construction had been adopted, Telford had built the Menai suspension bridge, the first iron steamship had been launched, the Stockton to Darlington railway had begun business. The list is long and ranges from the introduction of friction matches to Nelson's process for producing very high temperatures in blast furnaces. This proliferation stimulated cartoonists both to describe the industrial horrors of the time and to indulge in nightmarish visions of the future—some of which were peculiarly prophetic.

1

A View in the Whitechapel Road 1831, Anon (1828) A futuristic impression of the traffic (and pollution) problems to come. Steam carriages had already been tried with limited success. Although the artist has banished horses completely from these streets, the next year the first horse-drawn omnibus was to run in London.

2

London going out of Town, G. Cruikshank (1829) The kilns belch bricks and robot-like jerry builders put haystacks to flight, savage fences and trees as Hampstead encroaches further on the countryside. As towns absorbed more and more labour for the factories and mills, there was an urgent call for cheap, quick housing—and the slums were born.

3

March of Intellect, Heath (1829) In this fantastic medley of things-to-come there are: a vacuum-tube from Greenwich to Bengal, a suspension bridge from Bengal to Cape Town, a steam horse, a Royal Patent Boot Cleaning Engine, a flying machine for convicts to Australia and a flying postman.

1

LONDON going out of Town — or — The March of Bricks & Mortar.

2

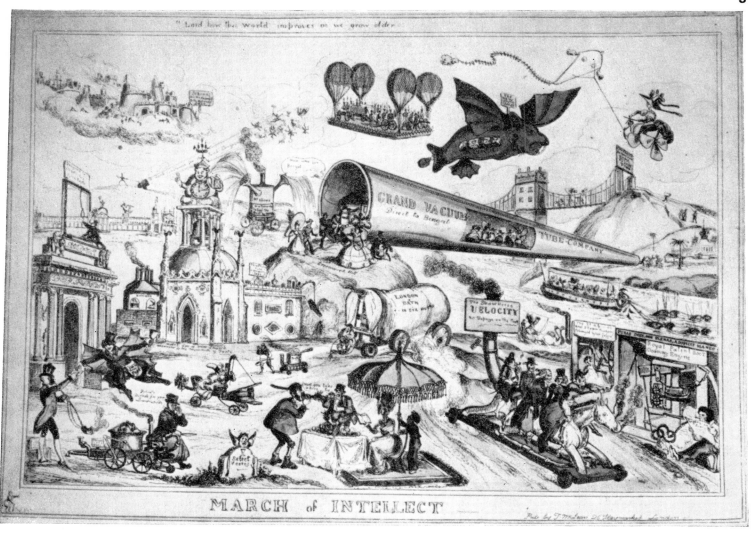

1830

SAILOR KING AHOY

George IV died of the dropsy in June and was succeeded by William IV, a very different kind of King whose general popularity somewhat inhibited the barbs of the cartoonists. For where George had been mocked for his self-indulgence and reviled for his posturing, William was the 'sailor king' and more sympathetic to his people (and, it was assumed, to reform). Against all expectations Wellington's ministry was not fired on the spot, but its image rapidly grew more and more tarnished; the severe recession of the year did not help nor the Duke's own obstinate attitude to the burning issue of the day, parliamentary reform. The end came unexpectedly over the relatively minor matter of the Civil List. Equally unexpectedly Grey's new Liberal-Whig ministry made no reductions in the Civil List either. The year ended with riots by disillusioned labourers, outbreaks of arson by the mysterious 'Captain Swing' and fierce sentences on the offenders.

1
Hokie Pokie Wankie Fum, Heath (1830) John Bull roasted by taxation and skewered by the Corn Bill is prepared as a feast for the cannibalistic government. Peel stirs the gravy while Wellington bastes the burnt offering. On to the scene rushes the new King determining to 'put a stop to this'.

2
The Civil List !!! Heath (1830) Grey's new ministry did not reduce the civil list, as expected. A Chelsea Pensioner, a farmhand and a sailor discuss the iniquity of it, while on the other side of an uncrossable canal a stream of fashionable ladies parade their pensions.

3
Merry England, Heath (1831) Public outcry against the severity of the punishment on rioters, who had burnt haystacks and destroyed machinery at the end of the year, is summed up by this disheartened print captioned 'Stands England where it did?'

HOKIE POKIE WANKIE FUM — *The King of the Cannibal Islands*

THE CIVIL LIST !!!

Stands England where it did

MERRY ENGLAND

4

The Real Swing, Anon (1832) Wellington represented to all reformers and radicals the old style of Tory, entrenched in defence of privilege. Here he is 'unmasked' as the infamous incendiary Captain Swing (supposedly the perpetrator of the outburst of rick-burning that was currently the scourge of the South of England).

5

The Brummagem Member, Heath (1830) In 1828 the Tories had refused to disenfranchise certain grossly corrupt boroughs and transfer the representation to the then unrepresented industrial cities of Manchester and Birmingham. Birmingham in particular became a stronghold of agitation for Parliamentary Reform after the founding there of Thomas Attwood's Political Union in January 1830. It is not recorded that its new members were eventually received in the House with such repugnance as envisaged here.

6

The Colossus, Seymour (1831) Brougham, a staunch advocate of Reform, was at the height of his popularity in 1830 when he was returned as Whig MP for Yorkshire. Grey promptly gave him a place in his ministry, made him Lord Chancellor and translated him to the Lords (where he caused no end of trouble). See also *The Political Toyman* (1825).

THE REAL SWING!!

THE BRUMMAGEM MEMBER

5

1831–1832
THE FIRST REFORM BILL

The battle for the First Reform Bill was fought as fiercely outside Parliament as inside. The Radicals and working class, spurred on by the successes of their French counterparts in the July Revolution (1830), stepped up their agitation, rioting, burning towns and countryside alike, and attacking the execrated 'borough-mongers' and the Lords and Bishops who were propping them up. The failure of Russell's first attempt to get the Bill through the Commons forced Grey to appeal to the country—and he was rewarded with a majority of 136. The next obstacle, the Lords, was made of sterner stuff, and even the winter of renewed rioting and terrorism that followed their rejection could not make them change heart. The King, watching his kingdom burn and the irresistible Grey opposed by the immovable Lords, appealed to Wellington to form a ministry and get the Bill through at all costs. But Wellington's days were over and within a week Grey was back, this time armed with a promise from the King to create enough new peers to outvote Tory opposition if necessary. That was enough. In June 1832 the Reform Bill became law, redistributed over 140 seats, and eliminated all antiquated forms of franchise.

1
Grey-vy Soup for the Poor, Heath (1831) The Reform Bill in its final manifestation still left vast areas of the population unfranchised. Its £10 a year qualifying limit excluded virtually all the working-class and gave rise to two more epic struggles for reform before the end of the century.

2
The Reaction in Bristol, Heath (1831) Serious unemployment and starvation in the country, coupled with anger at the Lords' rejection of the Bill, precipitated repeated outbreaks of mob violence. In Bristol the centre of the city was set on fire by Radicals.

3
Salus Populi Suprema Lex, G. Cruikshank (1832) The already acute distress was made worse in London by an outbreak of cholera. This and the 1848 outbreak (which gave rise to the Public Health Act of the same year) finally shamed corporations into attending to the appalling sanitary arrangements in cities.

1

2

1833–1837

THE MARCH OF REFORM

For three years following the Reform Bill the Whig ministry continued to reap a harvest of reforms, the first fruits of which they had tasted so sweetly in 1832. In 1833 the last act was performed in Wilberforce's long drama when slavery throughout the British Empire was abolished, the 1834 Poor Law attempted—not very equitably—to attend to some of the social evils exposed by the Royal Commission, and in 1835 local government reform followed parliamentary, establishing Councils to be elected by ratepayers. Under pressure from the working classes in the north the Factory Act of 1833 was passed, setting up factory inspectors and considerably reducing child-labour, but workers were left very much to help themselves, which they were in a mood to do. Robert Owen's attempt to create a grand National Trade Union failed from lack of organization, though it rallied and, to some extent, unified the working classes in defence of the Tolpuddle Martyrs (deported for forming an agricultural labourers' Union under oath). Meanwhile rent and tithe wars were raging in Ireland which, once Melbourne's new ministry in 1835 became dependent on O'Connell's support, could no longer be ignored. The Lords continued to hamper progressive legislation but they were persuaded to accept the commutation of tithes in 1837 and a degree of Irish municipal reform the next year.

1

Slavery and Freedom, Seymour (1833) Through the omissions of the Reform Bill and the emancipation of slaves, passed in 1833, the labourers in Britain were now technically no better off than the ex-slaves of the Empire.

2

Reform Bill's first step, Parry (1833) Although the passing of the Reform Bill only enfranchised a section of the middle class, it created a political monster—sovereignty of the people—which was soon to overwhelm the privileged minority that had been forced to bring it into existence.

3

The Operative builders, Grant (1834) Efforts in the early thirties to form trade unions were stubbornly resisted by employers, as was the attempt (depicted here) by the building workers to form an association. From such confrontations sprung the seeds of the Chartist Movement (begun by the London Working Men's Association in 1836).

1

2

4

Magisterial Justice, Grant (1834) In addition to the fate of the Tolpuddle Martyrs another *cause célèbre* of the labour movement was the arrest of Hector Hetherington (later a Chartist leader) for selling *The Poor Man's Guardian* without paying stamp tax.

5

The Reconciliation, Doyle (1835) By the Lichfield House Compact, a tacit agreement between the Irish leader in Parliament, Daniel O'Connell and the Whigs was made, whereby the Irish gave them support in Parliament and the Whigs voted against coercion acts. The following month, Peel's ministry (which was only in office through the King's intervention), was forced to resign.

THE RECONCILIATION.
AN AFFECTING SCENE.

1837–1841

VICTORIA AND MELBOURNE

Victoria succeeded to the throne on 18th June 1837 at the tender age of eighteen. From her uncle she inherited the continuing problems of Irish unrest, working-class aspirations towards franchise and an unpopular Whig ministry that had run out of its reforming zeal. Melbourne she liked personally but his majority was precarious. When, in 1839, it became so small he had to resign, she contrived to thwart Peel's effort to form a ministry by refusing to dismiss two of her Whig ladies-in-waiting at his request. But in 1841 there was nothing she could do about the unequivocable choice of Peel by the electors (by that time, however, she had found a closer companion in the Prince Consort). The people greeted her accession with delight, but there also coincided with the beginning of her reign two popular political movements which expressed the growing trend towards sovereignty of the people: in 1838 the People's Charter (demanding among other things manhood suffrage) was formulated by the Working Men's Association, and in Manchester the Anti-Corn Law League was established by Richard Cobden. Both were to affect the politics of the next decade.

1

The Queen in danger, Doyle (1837) The Queen quickly established an affectionate working relationship with her first Prime Minister, Melbourne (left)—much to the alarm of the Conservatives and Peel (right) who gibed that she was Queen of the Whigs, not of England.

2

Fishing Scene in Windsor Park, Foz (1839) Albert, younger son of the Duke of Saxe-Coburg, arrived on a visit to Windsor in October 1839. The Queen had, she confessed, viewed his visit with trepidation and announced to her relatives beforehand that there was no question of an engagement. On the 15th of October she announced her engagement.

3

The Dog in the manger, Doyle (1841) John Bull looks on in anticipation as Peel (the bull) comes to remove Melbourne (the dog) from the cosy resting-place he had enjoyed for so long and which, after the election of 1841, was no longer rightfully his.

1

2

FISHING SCENE IN WINDSOR PARK.
COMING EVENTS CAST THEIR SHADOWS BEFORE THEM.

ILLUSTRATION OF THE DOG IN THE MANGER,

1841–1845

FREE TRADE OR PROTECTION?

The first task facing Peel on his return to power was to repair the decrepit state of trade and the economy which the Whigs had let the country fall into. How to do it became an issue of the greatest intensity between the Free Traders who would abolish tariffs (and especially the Corn Laws) and the Protectionists who feared for the fortunes of the 'agricultural interests'. Peel himself over the period was converted to Free Trade and his budgets of 1842–45 were a step in that direction. But the repeal of the Corn Laws was an issue that threatened to bring the Government and People into direct conflict, for Cobden's Anti-Corn Law League had won over even manufacturers and was a political force to be reckoned with. A bad harvest in 1845, moreover, and the failure of the Irish potato crop made cheap corn a necessity for mere survival. The Whigs, secure in opposition came out for immediate repeal but Peel, while willing, was unable to carry his Cabinet on this issue. His resignation in December and Russell's refusal to form a ministry brought the Conservatives face to face with the crisis. With the help of Wellington in the Lords, Peel got his Repeal—but it split his party and kept it out of office for twenty years.

1

Caius Marius sitting amidst the ruins of Carthage, Doyle (1842)   Russell's Reform Bill was intended to be a final settlement of the public clamour for enfranchisement. By 1842 it was clear that it was only a beginning as one Chartist petition after another was presented to, and rejected by, Parliament.

2

The Race between the Hare and the Tortoise, Doyle (1843)   Peel (tortoise) was more gradual, if more consistent, in his conversion to Free Trade than Russell (hare), leader of the Opposition. Peel's budgets from 1842 had shown a steady movement in that direction. It was not until his famous Edinburgh Letter of November 1845 that Russell came out publicly in favour.

3

Extraordinary case of Nightmare, Doyle (1842)   Successive Whig budgets had shown an annual deficit. After reducing many duties and modifying the sliding scale to encourage import of corn, Peel had to pay his way by reviving income tax.

1

CAIUS MARIUS SITTING AMIDST THE RUINS OF CARTHAGE.

RACE BETWEEN THE HARE AND THE TORTOISE.

2

EXTRAORDINARY CASE OF NIGHT-MARE!

4
Rebecca and her daughters, Leech (1843) With the return of the Conservatives to power, O'Connell the Irish leader could no longer look to Parliament for assistance. Instead he began agitating at home in earnest for the Repeal of the Union—or as it came to be known, Home Rule.

5
The Nelson Testimonial, Grant (1844) What was derisively termed 'Nelson's lamp post' was not viewed with universal approval at a time when thousands were starving.

6
The Bull and the Frog, Leech (1844) Richard Cobden's Anti-Corn Law League succeeded as a grassroots political movement where Chartism failed. Its success in politically educating vast audiences evoked strong reactions from Protectionists and even would-be allies like *The Times*.

7
Finality, Doyle (1844), and

8
The Knave of Spades, Leech (1845) Two contemporary views of Peel's new brand of Liberal Conservatism; the first somewhat optimistic in prophesying the death of Whigism (it was to be the Conservatives who were snuffed out within two years), the second somewhat extravagant in its accusation of political cardsharping—though many of his own party were alienated by his *volte-face* on Protection. (The spade refers to a recent public engagement in which he had dug the first shovelful of a railway tunnel.)

146

REBECCA AND HER DAUGHTERS.

Tolltaker . . Sir R. P—l.   *Irish Rebecca* . . D——l O'C——l.   *Rebecca's Daughters* by Members of the Repeal Ass——n.

THE NELSON TESTIMONIAL!

5

THE ANTI-CORN-LAW LEAGUE AND THE ANTI-LEAGUE.

A NEW VERSION OF

THE BULL AND THE FROG.

A NEW READING TO THE POLITICAL PHRASE

FINALITY!

THE KNAVE OF SPADES.

1846–1848

THE DOWNFALL OF PEEL

The Corn Laws were abolished in June 1846, a triumph for Peel but also his downfall. The Conservatives were split from top to bottom by the decision, the Protectionists finding a passionate spokesman in Disraeli. Against the force of his invective Peel was unable to stay in control and, defeated over the passage of the Irish Coercion Bill in the Commons at the very moment his Repeal was passing through the Lords, he resigned in favour of a Liberal Government under Russell (with Palmerston as Foreign Secretary). The situation in Ireland turned from bad to worse as another potato-crop failure in 1846 followed hard on that of 1845 and the Government attempted to keep alive those whom it had formerly tried to coerce, and watched as Ireland was drained of its inhabitants by famine and emigration. It watched, too, as Europe tore itself apart in 'The Year of Revolutions' (1848) as state after state rose up against their military despots, and feared for war.

1
A Dangerous situation, Doyle (1846) In April of 1846 Peel found himself falling between the two stools of repealing the Corn Laws, which divided his party, and passing the Coercion Bill which gave the Liberals the chance they needed to defeat him in the Commons.

2
Stag at Bay, Doyle (1846) In this parody of Landseer's picture exhibited at the RA's exhibition, Peel (stag) faces his two most vehement critics over Free Trade, Bentinck (left) and Disraeli.

3
The Trojans petition Dido for Protection, Doyle (1846) The great bastion of Protectionism was the Lords and in particular the Conservative peers (here kneeling: the Dukes of Newcastle, Beaufort, Buckingham, Norfolk and Richmond). But because of Wellington's non-intervention (standing behind the Queen with Aberdeen and Graham) the Repeal passed through the House. Looking on are Bright, Cobden and Russell (left) and Peel (centre).

4
The Fall of Caesar, Doyle (1846) After his resignation in June Peel was never to hold office again. The conspirators left to right: Disraeli, Bentinck, Cobden, (in spite of having achieved, through Peel, the abolition of the Corn Laws) O'Connell, Russell, Lord Morpeth, Palmerston and Shiel.

1

A DANGEROUS SITUATION.

STAG AT BAY.
Suggested by the beautiful Picture of Edwin Landseer R.A. Esq. exhibited at the Royal Academy 1846.

2

THE TROJANS PETITION DIDO FOR "PROTECTION".

O Regina, novam cui condere Jupiter urbem,
Justitiaque dedit gentis frenare superbas.
Troes te miseri, ventis maria omnia vecti,
Oramus: prohibe infandos a navibus ignis:

Parce pio generi, et propius res adspice nostras.
Non nos aut ferro Libycos populare Penates
Venimus, aut raptas ad litora vertere praedas:
Non ea vis animo, nec tanta superbia victis.

THE FALL OF CAESAR.

5

Deaths by Starvation, Anon (1847)
Over half a million people in Ireland
died of famine or disease after two
successive failures of the potato crop.
In some cases absentee English land-
lords continued with their policy of
evicting starving tenants.

6

The Old Donkey turned restive at last,
Doyle (1848) With duty on so many
imports reduced or abandoned, Russell
found it necessary to continue the
trend of Conservative budgets by
increasing income tax.

7

The (modern) Deluge, Doyle (1848)
The Year of Revolutions: one after
another countries revolted against the
despotism of their governments. In
Naples, Paris, Venice, Berlin, Milan,
Vienna, Poland, the Danube and
Hungary popular insurrections were
either cooled by the promise of new
constitutions or suppressed (as during
the 'June Days' in Paris) with great
loss of life. The monarchies emerged
from the melée shaken and partially
modernized, but largely intact.

8

Lord John Russell 'at home', R. Doyle
(1847) Russell sits transfixed at the
bombardment of so many impending
and complicating issues.

9

*Ye Manners and ye Customs of ye
Englyshe*, R. Doyle (1849) Richard
Doyle's famous series was almost the
last work he did for *Punch* before re-
signing in protest at the magazine's
policy over Catholicism.

SERVANTS OF THE LORD, RENDERING AN ACCOUNT OF THEIR STEWARDSHIP DURING THE FAMINE OF 1847.

DEATHS BY STARVATION

THE OLD DONKEY TURNED RESTIVE AT LAST.

6

THE MODERN DELUGE.

LORD JOHN RUSSELL "AT HOME."

Yᵉ COMMONS RESSOLVED INTO A COMMYTTEE OF Yᵉ WHOLE HOVSE.

CHAPTER

VI

PRIME MINISTERS
AND THEIR
PARTIES

1846–1852
John Russell, Earl Russell (Whig)

1852
Edward Stanley, Earl of Derby (Tory)

1852–1855
*George Hamilton Gordon, Earl of Aberdeen
(Peelite)*

1855–1858
Henry Temple, Viscount Palmerston (Liberal)

1858
Edward Stanley, Earl of Derby (Conservative)

1858–1865
Henry Temple, Viscount Palmerston (Liberal)

1865–1866
John Russell, Earl Russell (Liberal)

1866–1868
Edward Stanley, Earl of Derby (Conservative)

1868
Benjamin Disraeli, Earl of Beaconsfield (Conservative)

1868–1874
William Gladstone (Liberal)

1874–1880
Benjamin Disraeli (Tory)

1880–1885
William Gladstone (Liberal)

1885–1886
*Robert Gascoyne-Cecil,
Marquess of Salisbury (Conservative)*

1886
William Gladstone (Liberal)

1886–1892
*Robert Gascoyne-Cecil,
Marquess of Salisbury (Conservative)*

CHAPTER VI

The first fifty years of Victoria's reign, political caricature was virtually monopolized by *Punch*, which set about the job in a thoroughgoing, well-informed, unobjectionable and essentially middle-class fashion. Its cartoons were pervaded with the values of the times: a certain paternalism towards the plight of the working man, but a horror towards his political aspirations; a sense of the inherent rectitude (usually) of Britain's policies towards foreigners, and no doubts at all of her standing in the world; and a sprinkling of prejudices against the likes of would-be emancipated women or insinuating papists.

So consistent were *Punch*'s stances that even its symbols became stereotyped and were inherited wholesale by succeeding political cartoonists. Leech's avuncular John Bull didn't differ in spirit or presence from Partridge's over fifty years later. Britannia devel-

John Leech

Sir John Tenniel

154

oped into a buxom young lady, independent and formidable when her hackles were up, and melodramatic in her postures of grief when national tragedy had struck. Not an endearing creature, but a substantial one.

Its leading political artists were formidable too, much respected (John Tenniel, 1820–1914, earned the first knighthood for cartooning in 1893) and of long tenure: John Leech was principal political cartoonist for twenty-three years, Tenniel for thirty-seven years. Even Linley Sambourne had worked for *Punch* for thirty years solidly before he succeeded Tenniel in 1901. Respectability, for better or worse, had overtaken caricature. Until Sambourne made use of the new photoengraving processes later in the century, all *Punch*'s cartoons were translated on to woodengravings. This, perhaps, as much as Tenniel's realistic and angular style gave the *Punch* cartoons of the Victorian era their stamp of unmistakable propriety.

Yet many of *Punch*'s characterizations of the great contemporary statesmen have an enduring quality: little Lord Johnny (Russell), busy about some reform or other like a mischievous schoolboy really too irresponsible to be carrying the cares of State; Palmerston often in some menial position belied by his aristocratic bearing; Gladstone patriarchal, imperious and humourless—but above all there was Dizzy. It was in its flirtation with Disraeli that *Punch* came nearest to what might be called disrespect. The colourful, mercurial, sartorial Disraeli appeared in enough guises (dramatic, balletic, fantastic, athletic, etc) to merit a collected edition of them after his death. Little wonder that after his death *Punch* trundled out Britannia to ululate over the national disaster.

1849–1853

THE POLICIES OF PALMERSTON

With the establishment of the Whig ministry one statesman now came into his own—Lord Palmerston at the Foreign Office. His aggressive foreign policies continually put him on a collision course, not only with the radical opposition but even with his own colleagues and the Queen (who eventually had to insist on seeing all his despatches first). Palmerston was voluble in defence of his policy and often managed to strike the right chord (as with his *Civis Romanus Sum* speech in 1850) with a jingoist public whose appetite for adventure was whetted by forty years of peace. In December 1851, however, he miscalculated in approving Napoleon's coup d'état and was forced to resign by Russell. His revenge came the following year when Russell was defeated over the Militia Bill and he was restored to his rightful position in Aberdeen's Coalition (December 1852), in time to ponder on Russia's expansionist ambitions in Eastern Europe and the threat to the Continent's theoretical balance of power.

1
The bottle-holder, Leech (1851) In his efforts to prevent a European War after the revolutions of 1848, Palmerston had appeared to play the role of second to some strange pugilists. He had persuaded the Piedmontese not to march against the Austrians, acquiesced in the invasion of Hungary by Russia, and condoned Napoleon's bloodthirsty *coup d'état* in France.

2
There's always something, Leech (1852) Cabinet opposition to Palmerston's independent policies came to a head when he displayed his unauthorized approval of Napoleon, and his resignation was demanded.

3
Little success of the Arts of Rome in England, Aram (1850) The re-establishment of the Roman Catholic hierarchy in Britain in 1850 was countered the next year by the Ecclesiastical Titles Act, preventing Catholic bishops from taking titles from territory within Britain. The Anglican Church was in the process of being invigorated under the inspiration of the Oxford Movement, by the series of Whig reforms and by the Christian Socialism teachings of Kingsley and Maurice.

1

THE "JUDICIOUS BOTTLE-HOLDER;"
Or, Downing Street Pet.

"BLESS YOU! IT'S ALL CHAFF—WON'T COME TO A FIGHT. OLD NICK'S GOT NO CONSTITOOTION—AND THEN I'M BOTTLE-HOLDER ON T' OTHER SIDE, TOO!"

THERE'S ALWAYS SOMETHING.

"I'M VERY SORRY, PALMERSTON, THAT YOU CANNOT AGREE WITH YOUR FELLOW SERVANTS; BUT AS I DON'T FEEL 'NCLINED TO PART WITH JOHN, YOU MUST GO, OF COURSE."

2

LITTLE SUCCESS OF THE *Arts* OF ROME
IN ENGLAND

157

4

Chancellor of the Exchequer coming down easy, Leech (1852) From February to December 1852 there was an interlude of Conservative government under Derby, during which Disraeli—by then having disengaged himself from the lost Protectionist cause—was Chancellor of the Exchequer.

5

Aberdeen smoking the pipe of peace, Leech (1853) Unlike Palmerston, the Prime Minister Aberdeen was a man of pacific temperament, who believed the peace of Europe lay in maintaining the *status quo*. But the temper of Europe—and the British people—was against him.

6

Imperial Piety, Cruikshank (1853) The growth of Russian imperialism had become apparent in Poland and Hungary in 1848. In April 1853 the Tsar claimed a protectorate over all Christian states within the Ottoman Empire and reinforced his claim by blowing Turkey's wooden frigates to pieces at the battle of Sinope in November. The colossal destruction made navies aware of the need for armour plating for battleships.

4

THE CHANCELLOR OF THE EXCHEQUER COMING DOWN EASY.

ABERDEEN SMOKING THE PIPE OF PEACE.

5

IMPERIAL Piety!

Designed Etched & Published by George Cruikshank

Sold by W. Tweedie 337 Strand & by all Book & Printsellers

Or, the Russian "Te Deum", for the Successful Slaughter, at Sinope.

1854–1856

THE CRIMEAN WAR

In March 1854 Britain and France concluded a treaty with Turkey and drifted into war with Russia, reaching the Crimean fortress of Sebastopol by autumn. From the very first engagement at Alma, where the army was victorious but its commanders failed to follow up the advantage, it was clear that the British regiments had lost none of their fighting spirit in forty years of peace but their leaders were distinguished only by their incompetence. The siege of Sebastopol dragged on for a year, with gallant, almost suicidal defensive actions being fought by the British at Balaclava and Inkerman. Throughout the bitter Crimean winter the soldiers sat and suffered the breakdown of supplies and transport, without tents, adequate food or medical supplies. Revelations of these appalling conditions finally roused public opinion enough to bring down Aberdeen's government and hand over conduct of the war to the more energetic Palmerston.

1
Charge of the Light Brigade, Leech (1854) News of the inconclusive victory at Balaclava was greeted with rapture in Britain—until the unnecessary loss of life transformed rapture into resentment against the military authorities.

2
Bits of iron from the Crimea, Leech (1855) The Victoria Cross was first awarded, as the highest military honour, for bravery in the Crimean War.

3
Spades are trumps, Leech (1855) The public was made aware of conditions at Sebastopol largely through reports in *The Times* from its war correspondent, William Russell. His exposures aroused public opinion just in time to bring down Aberdeen and save the army.

4
Giving the office, Leech (1854) Aberdeen's ministry fell in February 1855 after a winter of growing dissatisfaction with his war policy.

5
Grand military spectacle, Leech (1855) In the years between the Napoleonic Wars and the Crimea, the army under the Duke of Wellington (who died in 1842) had resolutely refused to improve its equipment, abolish its abuses or rethink its strategy. Its administration under Lord Raglan remained outdated, inefficient and small-minded.

160

ENTHUSIASM OF PATERFAMILIAS,
On Reading the Report of the Grand Charge of British Cavalry on the 25th.

"WELL, JACK! HERE'S GOOD NEWS FROM HOME. WE'RE TO HAVE A MEDAL."
"THAT'S VERY KIND. MAYBE ONE OF THESE DAYS WE'LL HAVE A COAT TO STICK IT ON!"

2

3

"GIVING THE OFFICE."

Knave R — H. "I SAY, ABBY, MY OLD-UN, THE VESTMINSTER SESSIONS IS FIXED FOR THE 12TH. IF YOU AIN'T PREPARED WITH YOUR DEFENCE, YOU'D BETTER CUT."

GRAND MILITARY SPECTACLE

1857–1859

MUTINY IN INDIA

After the resolution of affairs in the Crimea, Britain found herself in another Palmerstonian fracas—this time with China over the boarding and arrest of the *Arrow*, flying under a British flag (1856). Defeated in the House over this questionable adventure, Palmerston appealed to his friends the people, whose support at the polls encouraged him to prosecute the Chinese war with his accustomed vigour. Then in May 1857 came the news that the sepoys at Meerut had mutinied against British rule and two months later that women and children had been brutally massacred at Cawnpore. Brilliant campaigns by heavily-outnumbered British forces under Nicholson at the gates of Delhi, around the Residency at Lucknow under Lawrence, in the streets of Cawnpore under Campbell and in Central India under Rose prevented the Mutiny spreading to the loyal, but wavering South. But before peace had officially returned to India Palmerston's popularity took a challenging knock over his handling of the Orsini Affair; Tories, Peelites, Russellites and Radicals all combined to oust him in favour of Derby. Poor Lord Derby (fated to be Prime Minister three times with three of the shortest ministries of the nineteenth century) barely managed to improve on his ten month administration of 1852 and in June 1859 handed the reins back to Palmerston, Russell and Gladstone ('the Triumvirate').

1

Execution of 'John Company', Leech (1857) After the mutiny many administrative changes were made in India, among them the abolition of the long-obsolete East India Company and the transferring of its powers to the Crown.

2

The Clemency of Canning, Leech (1858) The enlightened administration of Lord Canning, Governor-General in India, in setting a limit on reprisals in the aftermath of the Mutiny lost him much popularity at home.

3

The Derby—the return, Leech (1859) The brief interlude of Derby's government after Palmerston's fall was rudely curtailed by his failure to obtain a majority in the General Election of 1859.

4

The street up again, Leech (1859) Two months before his inevitable resignation in June, Derby's ministry had been defeated in the House over Disraeli's proposed Reform Bill.

162

1

EXECUTION OF "JOHN COMPANY;"

The Blowing up (there ought to be) in Leadenhall Street.

THE CLEMENCY OF CANNING.

GOVERNOR-GENERAL. "WELL, THEN, THEY SHAN'T BLOW HIM FROM NASTY GUNS; BUT HE MUST PROMISE TO BE A GOOD LITTLE SEPOY."

2

THE DERBY—THE RETURN.

JOHN BULL. "NOW THEN, SHOW YOUR TICKET! THREE HUNDRED AND TWO! YOU CAN'T GET THROUGH WITH THAT!"

1860–1863

THE TRIUMVIRATE

The Triumvirate which came into power in mid-1859 (Palmerston as Prime Minister, Russell as Foreign Secretary and Gladstone as Chancellor of the Exchequer) narrowly avoided becoming involved in other people's wars on three occasions. First the question of Italian unity, which the French Emperor abhorred and Russell, in particular, devoutly wished. Only by a refusal to send the British Fleet, with the French, to Messina was Garibaldi enabled to cross the Straits into Italy (August 1860). Then, in the next year, came the American Civil War, in which the inclinations of the upper reaches of British society (and Mr Gladstone) were with the South, if not actually with slavery. Two incidents particularly alienated the goodwill of the North: the Trent Affair in 1861, and the Alabama case in 1862. The latter—a Southern privateer had been allowed to escape from Liverpool Docks and inflicted some 15 million dollars' worth of damage on Northern shipping—left a ten-year legacy of bitterness and wrangling over reparations. And then, the Danish debacle in 1863. Denmark's annexation of Schleswig forced Britain, as her ally, to attempt a compromise with Austria and Prussia and 'blood & iron' Bismarck. If Denmark had to fight, said Palmerston, she would not fight alone. But fight alone she did, for Britain had neither the allies nor the resources to intervene in Europe.

1

The Next Invasion, Leech (1860) Instead of coming to blows with Emperor Napoleon III over Italian unity, the affair ended with a lucrative commercial treaty between Britain and France, engineered by Cobden. Under the terms of the treaty British coal was exported free of duty and French wine imported on cheaper terms.

2

The new Russell Six-pounder, Leech (1860) In March Lord Russell introduced a plan for Parliamentary Reform lowering the franchise qualification to £6. It was very coldly received, and it was to be another seven years before any progress was made.

3

The Lion of the Season, Leech (1861) Darwin's *Origin of Species* had appeared in 1859 and by now had become the talking-point of London.

THE NEXT INVASION.
LANDING OF THE FRENCH (LIGHT WINES) AND DISCOMFITURE OF OLD GENERAL BEER.

THE NEW RUSSELL SIX-POUNDER.

THE LION OF THE SEASON.

ALARMED FLUNKEY. "*Mr. G-g-g-o-o-o-rilla!*"

4

Look out for Squalls, Leech (1861) Two Southern representatives who had been sent to England to try to rally Britain to the Confederate cause were removed from an English boat, *The Trent*, by the North. It might have precipitated Britain into the war had it not been for the mediation of Prince Albert and the peaceable nature of Russell.

5

The Parliamentary Python, Leech (1862) Parliamentary business had been discarded during the Trent crisis, like the eggs (numbering 100) of a pythoness at the London Zoo which had addled while she was busy discarding her skin. (Left: Palmerston and Russell. Right: Disraeli.)

6

Dundreary Row, Leech (1862) The fashionable class of gent at the time was the 'swell', whose whiskers and dress were modelled on Lord Dundreary, a character in a popular play.

7

Europa carried off by the (John) Bull, Tenniel (1863) In 1863 Napoleon III proposed a Congress of Europe 'to arrive at the pacification of Europe'. The Government rejected the idea, suspicious of Napoleon's ambitions to be supreme in Europe. The Congress was ultimately called off.

THE PARLIAMENTARY PYTHON.

5

DUNDREARY ROW—HYDE PARK.

Said one DUNDREARY to another DUNDREARY—" By Jove! It's awfully jolly; ain't it?"

EUROPA CARRIED OFF BY THE (JOHN) BULL.

1864–1866
RUN-UP TO REFORM

The death of Lord Palmerston in 1865 and the succession of Lord Russell was the cue for another assault on Parliamentary Reform. Like the Bill of 1832, the Second Reform Bill was preceded by the snowballing of popular agitation—this time encouraged by the success of the North in the American Civil War and led by John Bright whose rallies would sometimes reach 200,000-strong. Russell's attempt at legislation in 1866, however, was a half-hearted affair (proposing a £7 rather than a household suffrage) and was quickly despatched by the Conservatives and forty diehard Whigs (dubbed 'Adulamites'). Russell resigned as he was honourably bound to do, giving way to a Conservative ministry under Lord Derby and Disraeli. The fact that there was still a problem in Ireland, largely forgotten since the Famine, was suddenly and forcibly brought to the attention of the new administration by an outburst of Fenian outrages. The Fenians began attacking police barracks in Ireland, then turned their attention on London and Manchester. Mr Gladstone's attention, if no one else's, was caught.

1

Moses starting for the Conference Fair, Leech (1864)   Lord Russell (as Moses from *The Vicar of Wakefield*) prepares for the London Conference, April 1864, on the Danish Question (see previous page). Through Bismarck's astuteness nothing whatever was achieved and the war was resumed two months later.

2

The False Start, Tenniel (1864)   To everyone's surprise, and not least Lord Palmerston's, Mr Gladstone came out in a Parliamentary debate in May in favour of a very wide extension of the franchise.

3

Pegasus Unharnessed, Tenniel (1865) Gladstone's embracing of franchise reform lost him his University seat at Oxford in the general election. He immediately took over a more appropriate constituency in Lancashire, considering himself 'unmuzzled' at last.

MOSES STARTING FOR THE CONFERENCE FAIR.
(LET US HOPE HE WON'T BRING BACK "A GROSS OF GREEN SPECTACLES.")

Primrose . . . PALMERSTON.   Mrs. Primrose . . . BRITANNIA.   Moses . . . EARL RUSSELL.

THE FALSE START.
PAM (The Starter). "Hi! Gladstone! Democracy! Too soon! too soon! You musn't go yet!"

PEGASUS UNHARNESSED.

4

The Fenian-Pest, Tenniel (1866)
Fenian troubles throughout Ireland early in the year brought about the suspension of Habeas Corpus. The next year a Fenian explosion in Clerkenwell killed twelve people and injured another 100. In Manchester a policeman was shot dead when two Fenian prisoners were rescued from a prison van. The perpetrators were hanged and became known as the Manchester martyrs.

5

Queen Hermione, Tenniel (1865)
Since the death of the Prince Consort (in 1861) the Queen had lived in remote retirement and neglected her public duties—as she was to continue to do for some years.

6

The Working-man, Tenniel (1865)
In 1865 a Bill to reduce the franchise from £10 to £6 was introduced by a Mr Baines. The resulting debate stimulated some very personal portraits of the working-man. John Bright, the champion of universal suffrage, envisaged him as the angelic artisan whose only sustenance need be pure water. At the other extreme, Robert Lowe (the leader of the Adulamites, who opposed any change in the law at all) denounced him as a time-wasting sot whose only pursuit was the swilling of beer.

4

THE FENIAN-PEST

Hibernia: 'O my dear Sister, what ARE we to do with these troublesome people?'

Britannia: 'Try isolation first, my dear, and then———'

5

THE WORKING-MAN, FROM THE ROYAL WESTMINSTER EXHIBITION.

1867

SECOND REFORM BILL

Disraeli, even had he wanted to, could not have ignored the popular support Bright's campaign for Reform received over the winter of 1866. Ever the opportunist, Disraeli introduced a new Bill based on a ratepaying franchise, hoping to please both Conservatives and Reformers, but at the same time hedging it about with safeguards which effectively emasculated it. By the time it had gone through the Committee stage, Gladstone and Bright had so whittled away these safeguards that the Bill emerged virtually as household suffrage for the boroughs (in the counties it included landowners worth £5 a year and tenants paying £12). The Bill was passed, with surprisingly little rearguard resistance, on August 15. The immediate effect of the Bill, of course, was to bring Gladstone and the Liberals back into power in the following year's election.

1
The Brummagem Frankenstein, Tenniel (1866) In the North, Reform demonstrations were massively supported—one in Birmingham reportedly attracted a quarter of a million people. John Bright was nearly always the principal speaker on such occasions.

2
A Leap in the Dark, Tenniel (1867) Disraeli (the horse) takes Britannia into the thickets of Reform without knowing where either of them will land. The title of this cartoon was used by Lord Derby in the Lords on the passing of the Bill (to the delight of *Punch*).

3
The Road to Sheffield, Tenniel (1867) Trade Unionism had begun to attract much unfavourable public attention. Lacking as it did any political organization, it often resorted to violent acts of intimidation against recalcitrant workers. The blowing-up of a worker's house in Sheffield in 1866 aroused great public indignation and, in the following year, a judgment against the Boilermakers' Union seemed to render unions illegal.

4
Pounded!, Tenniel (1868) The sequel to *A Leap in the Dark*. Gladstone helps Britannia onto a fresh mount (the Liberal Party), while Disraeli (who lost the election following the passing of the Reform Bill) flounders in a bog.

1

THE BRUMMAGEM FRANKENSTEIN.

JOHN BRIGHT. "*I have no fe-fe-fear of Ma-Manhood Suffrage!*"—MR. BRIGHT's Speech at Birmingham.

A LEAP IN THE DARK.

2

THE ROAD TO SHEFFIELD

Punch: '*Now, then, stop that, I say! We'll have no intimidation here.*'

"POUNDED!"

The Result of the "Leap in the Dark."

[See *Punch* for August 3, 1867.

1868–1871
SOCIAL PROGRESS

With the passing of the Reform Bill, the House was in the mood for more. Within a week the Conservatives had added two new Acts to the statute book which considerably improved factories and conditions of work for women and children. But with the début of Mr Gladstone's first ministry, Parliament was positively infused with a reforming zeal. The disestablishment of the Irish Church in 1869 removed a continuing grievance, and the Irish Land Act of 1870 provided some measure of compensation for evicted peasants. In that year and the next, laws were passed giving wives greater power over their own property, allowing students to enter Oxbridge without religious tests, legalizing trade unions, setting up local government boards, and the most far-reaching of them all, the Education Act, providing for universal primary education.

1

Rival Actors, Tenniel (1868) At the general election it was widely recognized that though the Reform Bill had passed under Disraeli's name, what had emerged was in essence Gladstone's policy.

2

A Change for the better, Tenniel (1869) The bringing to an end of the civil establishment of the Church in Ireland amounted to the most important ecclesiastical revolution since Tudor times.

3

John Bright's new Reform Bill, Tenniel (1870) With his Quaker convictions and from his new elevated position in the Cabinet, Bright continued to exhort the working-class to the popular ideal of Self-help (which included, of course, giving up drink).

4

The Political Egg-dance, Tenniel (1867) It was one of the consequences of Disraeli's Reform Bill that the newly-enfranchised voters greatly increased the radical representation in the Liberal Party.

RIVAL ACTORS

(Mr Gladstone, as William Tell, has been called before the curtain 'amid the deafening plaudits of a house crammed to the ceiling'.)
Mr Bendizzy (Jeremy Diddler): 'He's got the house with him, that's certain. Ahem! I must give 'em a touch of my ART.'

A CHANGE FOR THE BETTER

Ghost of Queen Elizabeth: 'Agreed, have they? Ods Boddikins! God's my life, and marry come up, Sweetheart! In MY time I'd have knocked all their addlepates together till they HAD agreed!'

THE POLITICAL EGG-DANCE.

5

Obstructives, Tenniel (1870) The passage of the Education Act was marked by vehement Nonconformist protests that state grants to Church schools were being doubled to enable them to become a permanent part of the system.

6

The Strong Government, Tenniel (1871) By the summer of 1871 so many Government measures had been modified or abandoned that the Opposition twitted them that all they would have to show for the whole session was the Ballot Bill.

7

An Ugly Rush, Tenniel (1870) An optimistic effort in May to extend the franchise to women was defeated by a substantial majority. Some concession was made to women in August with the Married Women's Property Act, but the scent of emancipation was in the air (both Girton and Newnham colleges for women were founded at this time).

5

"OBSTRUCTIVES."

MR. PUNCH (to BULL A 1). "Yes, it's all very well to say, 'Go to School!' How are they to go to School with those people quarrelling in the doorway? Why don't you make 'em move on?"

THE STRONG GOVERNMENT.

BEN (a rude boy). "Now, then, all together!—and be very careful as you don't overdo yerselves!"

6

AN "UGLY RUSH!"

MR. BULL. "Not if I know it!"

See Division on the Woman's Vote Bill.

1872–1875

MR GLADSTONE AND MR DISRAELI

The stirrings of Liberal disunity became apparent in March 1873 when forty-three of his own party voted against Gladstone's Irish University Bill. But with Disraeli unwilling to take office with a minority, Gladstone soldiered on until the general election in February 1874. Had he won, he might have abolished income tax (as he was proposing). Income tax is still with us, however, for Disraeli swept into office with the first clear Conservative majority since 1841. For the first time since the death of Palmerston the voice of Britain was to be heard to some effect in Europe and further afield.

1

The Two Augurs, Tenniel (1873) The conflict, not just of policies but of personality and rhetoric, between Disraeli and Gladstone added glamour and distinction to the House. It also gave a scope to the cartoonists which they had not enjoyed since the rivalry of Fox and Pitt.

2

A Friend in Need, Tenniel (1873) Bright's appointment to Chancellor of the Duchy of Lancaster coincided with the outbreak of the Ashanti War. There was much speculation as to whether his Peace principles would force him to oppose the war.

3

Home-(rule)-opathy, Tenniel (1874) In June Mr Butt (opposed, as it happened, by Dr Ball for the Government) presented his cure for Irish troubles, Home Rule. It was crushingly defeated.

4

Great Autumn manoeuvre, Tenniel (1873) An important section of the nation which had not benefited from the Reform Bill was the agricultural workers. In July 1873 an attempt was made (with Gladstone's wholehearted support) to extend household franchise to the counties. It was 'talked out' of Parliament and had to wait until 1884. The following year (1874) there was a seven month strike by agricultural workers in south-east England, but throughout the seventies attempts, such as Joseph Arch's Agricultural Labourers' Union (1872), to improve their conditions were doggedly suppressed.

1

A FRIEND IN NEED.

2

HOME-(RULE)-OPATHY.

IRELAND. *"Ah, sure, thin, it's cruel bad I am, intirely; and it's the dacent Gentleman here knows the stuff to do me good!"*
DR. BULL. *"No, no, Friend BUTT!—None of your nostrums! We saw her well through the 'Repeal' Fever,—and she'll come out of this all right yet!"*

GREAT AUTUMN MANOEUVRE

Hodge: 'Lor-a-massy, Me-aster! Be oi to be a "Power in t' Ste-ate"? What be oi to get by tha-at?'

Mr G: 'That, my good friend, is a mere detail. The question is, what am I to get by it!!'

"In the Debate as to giving a vote to the Agri-cultural Labourer, Mr Forster read a letter from the Premier, who declared that such extension of franchise was just and politic and could not be avoided. The question was thus taken up by the Government, which much needs a 'good cry'."

GREAT AUTUMN MANŒUVRE.

5

Neptune's warning, Tenniel (1875)
Two naval tragedies, the sinking of the
Vanguard in September and the near-
sinking of the *Iron Duke* in November,
drew the public's attention to the un-
seaworthiness of Britain's iron-clad
fleet and the working conditions of
sailors in these 'coffin boats'. Legislation to improve these was begun by
Samuel Plimsoll the next year.

6

Mose in Egitto!!! Tenniel (1875) The
purchase of Suez Canal shares at the
end of this year was the beginning of
Britain's long and tortuous involve-
ment in Egypt. At the time Disraeli saw
it as only serving the interests of the
Indian Empire and trade.

7

Paradise and the Peri, Tenniel (1874)
Disraeli returned to office in February
with a majority of eighty-three, the
first Conservative leader since Peel to
have such an undiluted luxury.

5

NEPTUNE'S WARNING.

FATHER NEP. *"Look here, my Lass! You used to 'Rule the Waves;' but if you* MIS-RULE *'em, as you've done lately, by Jingo there'll be a row!!!"*

BRITANNIA. *"I'm sure I don't know who's to blame, Papa dear!"*

FATHER NEP. *"Don't know!!! Then Pipe all Hands, and find out!!!"*

"MOSÉ IN EGITTO!!!"

6

PARADISE AND THE PERI.

"Joy, joy for ever ! my task is done—
The gates are passed, and Heaven is won ! "—LALLA ROOKH.

1876–1878

EMPRESS AND EARL

All eyes looked to the East in 1876, and none more anxiously than Disraeli's. An inquiry into Egypt's finances led in November to the establishment of dual control over that country by France and Britain (to safeguard their interests in the Canal). The tottering, and largely corrupt, Ottoman Empire in Europe was being threatened by Russia's imperialist ambitions. Disraeli's espousal of the Turkish cause—vigorously attacked by Gladstone—brought Britain to the brink of another Crimean War on more than one occasion: in May 1877 a stiff warning had to be sent to Russia against any attempted blockade of the Suez Canal; in June a Cabinet resolution was made to declare war should Russia occupy Constantinople; and in January and February 1878 the fleet was shuttled to and from the Straits in an agony of indecision. 'Jingoist' war fever gripped the country, but by July the Great Powers were assembled around a table in Berlin and thrashed out what Disraeli memorably was to call a 'Peace with Honour'.

1
Save only his Goosequill, Anon (1876) Stephen Cave, who was sent to examine Egypt's financial position after Britain's purchase of the Khedive's shares in the Suez Canal Company.

2
New Crowns for Old, Tenniel (1876) The Bill for adding to the Royal Titles that of 'Empress of India' met with very little public approval . . .

3
Empress and Earl, Tenniel (1876) . . . except perhaps Her Majesty's. Four months later Disraeli was elevated to the peerage with the title of Earl of Beaconsfield.

4
The Liliput levy on John Bull Gulliver, Anon (1876) There were many who found Disraeli's hectic foreign policy tiresome and objected to British taxes going towards propping up an empire of 'liliputan' Turks.

1

"NEW CROWNS FOR OLD ONES!"

(ALADDIN *adapted.*)

EMPRESS AND EARL;
OR, ONE GOOD TURN DESERVES ANOTHER.
LORD BEACONSFIELD. *"Thanks, your Majesty. I might have had it before! Now I think I have EARNED it!"*

THE LILIPUT LEVY ON JOHN BULL GULLIVER.

5
The Sweet Rose and the Prickly Thistle, CH (1876)   The Queen's prolonged seclusion at Balmoral, after the death of Prince Albert, and her reliance on her confidential servant John Brown (right) were constantly the subject of idle gossip and censorious newspaper articles.

6
Kaiser-i-Hind, Sambourne (1877)   On the 1st of January the Queen was proclaimed Empress of India in Delhi to assembled Maharajas, Nawabs, Nizams, etc, who duly affirm their continuing loyalty to the Crown.

7
The Man in Possession, Tenniel (1877)   In May Britain sent a despatch to Russia warning her against any attempt to blockade the Canal or occupy Egypt.

8
The Edison Light, Keene (1878)   The imminent application of electric light for domestic use in place of gas had caused great alarm among the holders of gas shares. This year also saw the birth of the carbon filament lamp and, apropos of this cartoon, the Eddystone Lighthouse.

5

THE SWEET ROSE—ENGLAND, 1837.   THE PRICKLY THISTLE—SCOTLAND, 1876.

KAISER-I-HIND.

6

THE MAN IN POSSESSION.

THE EDISON LIGHT.

(AND THE SILLY BIRDS.)

1879–1880

THE LIBERALS RETURN

Peace with honour did not mean that Britain was at peace everywhere. In Africa she was involved in a bloody campaign against the Zulus and, after the massacre of the British Legation at Kabul, an Afghan War. The Transvaal Boers, too, declared themselves independent of Britain and were preparing for the worst. Meanwhile Mr Gladstone up in his new constituency of Midlothian was roundly castigating the Government for its imperialism and mis-handling of home affairs—to very good effect. Times were indeed bad at home, with agriculture severely depressed. Beaconsfield determined on a snap election at Easter 1880, ostensibly on the issue of Irish Relief. The verdict, which had little to do with Ireland, was a colossal majority of 159 for the Liberals over the Conservatives. Beaconsfield died exactly a year later, in retirement.

1
Despise not your enemy, Tenniel (1879) The Zulu War began with a disaster for British forces at Isandhlwana and was followed by others. It was felt these were due to underestimating the enemy's strength.

2
The Colossus of Words, Tenniel (1879) Gladstone's election campaign in Midlothian ('his pilgrimage of passion' as it was described) aroused much admiration in the country—not so much for his denunciation of the Government as for his habit of delivering speeches at any time and in any place, even from the windows of railway trains. It was, in effect, Britain's first whistlestop tour.

3
The choice of Hercules, Tenniel (1880) Gladstone's first ministry had been primarily concerned with domestic reform, Disraeli's with foreign prestige.

4
The European Concert, Tenniel (1880) On taking office Gladstone announced he had every intention of acting 'in concert' with other European Powers over the Eastern Question—which basically meant coming to terms with Russia (on the drums), Bismarck (on the tuba) and Turkey (cymbals).

THE COLOSSUS OF WORDS.

THE CHOICE OF HERCULES.

THE "EUROPEAN CONCERT."

1881–1884

EGYPT, IRELAND AND SOUTH AFRICA

The Liberals, on their return to power, found themselves dragged into three conflicts for which neither they nor the pacific Mr Gladstone were prepared. The rising of the Boers in January 1881 shocked them into an immediate concession of independence. The vengeance of the Mahdi in the Sudan was the very thing they were trying to avoid by the removal of all Egyptian garrisons from the country—a more diplomatic man than General Gordon might have accomplished it. In Ireland the outrages were partly the result of their own repressive measures: in response to their Coercion Bill for Ireland (1881) there followed 2,590 agrarian outrages in a single year, the murder of the Irish Chief Secretary in Phoenix Park, obstructionist tactics in Parliament by Parnell's Home Rule Party, the rise of The Invincibles (a secret terrorist society), and bomb outrages in London—including one at the offices of *The Times*. Among all these brickbats their one bouquet was earned by the passing of the Third Reform Bill (1884) which brought about uniform suffrage in counties and boroughs.

1

The Bill-sticker, Tenniel (1881) Gladstone rightly insisted on the precedence of the Irish Land Bill over all other legislation, hoping that it would assuage the terrorists. Any effect it might have had, however, was negated by the continuance of coercion and the locking-up of Parnell, who had been to some extent a restraining influence.

2

The Two Memnons jointly noting, Sambourne (1882) There had been nationalist stirrings in Egypt the previous year when a native army had revolted and fifty Europeans killed in the subsequent revolution. Britain and France immediately sent a 'note' to the Khedive assuring him of support, but it was ultimately left to a British army under Wolseley to save Egypt from anarchy.

3

What will he grow to? Tenniel (1881) Edison and Swan had both independently invented a practical electric light for domestic use in 1880 and the streets of New York were lit by electricity for the first time. In 1881 Fauré demonstrated how electricity could be stored in a battery, and the next year the first hydroelectric plant was to go into operation.

THE BILL-STICKER.

THE TWO MEMNONS—JOINTLY NOTING.

2

"WHAT WILL HE GROW TO?"

4

Hopes and Fears, Sambourne (1882)
This year a scheme for a Channel Tunnel was mooted. Lord Grosvenor (mole on the left) spoke ardently in favour, Wolseley (the timid hare) argued against it on the grounds that it would encourage an invasion.

5

The Anglo-Indian Mutiny, Tenniel (1883) The Queen's Proclamation in 1880 had held out the promise of 'equal rights' to the natives. To the extreme indignation of the European British subjects they discovered that this would mean the possibility of being tried by a native magistrate. A truly British compromise was worked out: they would be allowed a majority white jury under a native magistrate.

6

Follow my leader, Tenniel (1884) Although the Third Reform Bill passed through the Commons with little opposition, the Lords—under the influence of Lord Salisbury (soon to be leader of the next Conservative Government)—vetoed it until a redistribution of seats should first be passed.

190

4

HOPES AND FEARS; OR, A DREAM OF THE CHANNEL TUNNEL.

THE ANGLO-INDIAN MUTINY.

(A BAD EXAMPLE TO THE ELEPHANT!)

"FOLLOW MY LEADER!"

1884

These plates, selected from a series of eight parodies on Hogarth's *Rake's Progress*, were originally published in *St Stephen's Review*, when Gladstone's second ministry had run for four years.

1
Rake's Progress, Tom Merry (1884) A new suit for the Rake (Gladstone) is being measured by his tailor (Joseph Chamberlain), when up comes Mrs Midlothian (Gladstone's constituency) to demand of the Rake that he redeem the promises made to her daughter in his electoral campaign of 1879 (in which he attacked the Tories for imperialism). Behind Gladstone lurk his constant bogeymen—Parnell whose obstructing of parliamentary business had made policy-making an uncomfortable business, and a Boer who had despaired of ever winning his promised self-government from Gladstone and had achieved it by force of arms.

2
The Rake's Levée, Gladstone, as in Hogarth's second plate, is surrounded by artists and professors. But in this version Chamberlain is the dancing master, Parnell the fencing master. Granville, the foreign secretary tries out his French Horn while Hartington kneels before him in the guise of a jockey. Next to Gladstone in the cocked hat stands Bradlaugh, the atheist member for Northampton (the Blasphemer) who was supported by Gladstone when he refused to take the religious oath in Parliament and was reviled for years to come. Gladstone himself holds a copy of one of his own poems—he was particularly fond of translating the classics.

3
In the Debtor's Prison, The jailor, Stafford Northcote (right), the leader of the parliamentary Opposition, has let in the Rake's wife (Britannia) (centre), to nag at him and his mistress (Midlothian) to come and plead with him. Midlothian is having to be revived by Mrs Chamberlain and Bright. On the table sits a letter from Salisbury (Conservative leader in the Lords) refusing to allow the passage of Gladstone's Reform Bill without an accompanying Bill to redistribute seats. A pot-boy (Lord Rosebery, who was to succeed Gladstone as leader of the Liberals) has brought the Rake a drink, but is demanding payment for it first, which the Rake of course is unable to provide.

4
The Madhouse, The Rake expires in the arms of Midlothian who, even in this extremity, has not deserted him. The keeper, Salisbury, shackles his legs. All Gladstone's colleagues have had to be committed to the madhouse, too, each afflicted with his own peculiar insanity.

1

2

1885–1887

THE IRISH QUESTION

For the next three years British politics was monopolized by the Irish Question, as Governments came and went on the issue. Lord Salisbury's brief Conservative ministry seemed at one point to be veering towards a compromise with the Home Rule party —or so it seemed, after an interview with the Conservative Viceroy of Ireland, to Parnell, who promptly called on all the Irish in Britain to vote Conservative in the 1885 election. He was mistaken. Salisbury's administration continued (only through its Irish Alliance, for the Liberals were only five short of an overall majority) but showed no sign whatever of satisfying Parnell. At that point Gladstone decided to grasp the nettle, committed himself to Home Rule, allied himself with Parnell and ousted the Government. In April 1886 he introduced his Home Rule Bill (unfortunately making no provisions for a separate Ulster). Three months later it had been thrown out of the Commons, his party was split down the middle (even Bright and Chamberlain voting with the Opposition), and a General Election—fought specifically on the issue—lost quite decisively. Except for one brief interlude Conservatives and Unionists were to rule Britain for the next twenty years.

1

The Jolly Anglers, Sambourne (1886) The Home Rule election exposed some strange alignments of loyalties. There were the Gladstonian Liberals (such as Harcourt, left) who supported Home Rule, Traditional Whigs (such as Lord Hartington, foreground) who hated the idea, Radical Whigs (like Chamberlain, with monocle) who disapproved of the terms of the Bill, and Conservatives (like Lord Randolph Churchill) who were pledged to support the Liberal Unionists. It was also agreed that no Conservative should contest the seat of a Unionist.

2

The Old Umbrella, Tenniel (1886) The Liberal leader's attempt to rally all shades of party opinion under what Lord Rosebery called the 'Gladstonian umbrella' proved hopeless. The Liberal party was in tatters.

3

As You Like It, Sambourne (1886) Having ousted Salisbury's government by allying himself to Parnell, Gladstone dispelled any doubts about his intentions on Home Rule by appointing John Morley, a fervent Home Ruler, to the Irish Secretaryship.

1

THE JOLLY ANGLERS.

CHURCHILL (to CHAMBERLAIN). "I say, old Fellow, we won't interfere with one another's Swims."
HARCOURT (with "Gladstone" lob-worm). "I think the Grand Old Bait will catch 'em."

THE "OLD UMBRELLA".

2

"AS YOU LIKE IT."

ORLANDO-MORLEY (about to grapple with Terrorism in Ireland). "*I come but in, as others do, to try with him the Strength of my Youth.*"

ROSALIND HIBERNIA. "*Now, Hercules be thy speed, young Man!*"

4
Sowing Tares, Tenniel (1886) In 1881 the Social Democratic Federation had been formed and made some headway in the Trade Union movement. In 1883 the Fabian Society was born and began to bring more intimate pressure to bear in government circles. This cartoon was occasioned by a riot in Trafalgar Square which was laid at the door of the 'Revolutionary Social Democratic League'.

5
Window studies, Du Maurier (1887)

6
A Jubilee Council of Past Masters, Keene (1887)

7
Peaceful triumphs of the reign, Sambourne (1887) Queen Victoria's Diamond Jubilee evoked a plethora of commemorative and congratulatory cartoons, as patriotic as only Victorian cartoonists could make them.

SOWING TARES.

(With a thousand apologies to Sir JOHN E. MILLAIS, Bart., R.A.)

SALVAM FAC REGINAM IMPERATRICEM

WINDOW STUDIES.
"THE HEAVENS LAUGH WITH YOU IN YOUR JUBILEE!" — WORDSWORTH.

5

A JUBILEE COUNCIL OF "PAST MASTERS".

PEACEFUL TRIUMPHS OF THE REIGN.

CHAPTER
VII

PRIME MINISTERS
AND THEIR
PARTIES

1886–1892
Robert Gascoyne-Cecil,
Marquess of Salisbury (Conservative)

1892–1894
William Gladstone (Liberal)

1894–1895
Archibald Primrose, Earl of Rosebery (Liberal)

1895–1902
Robert Gascoyne-Cecil,
Marquess of Salisbury (Conservative)

1902–1905
Arthur Balfour (Conservative)

1905–1908
Sir Henry Campbell-Bannerman (Liberal)

1908–1915
Herbert Asquith, Earl of Oxford and Asquith (Liberal)

1915–1916
Herbert Asquith (Coalition)

1916–1922
David Lloyd George, Earl of Dufor (Coalition)

CHAPTER VII

Will Dyson

Harry Furniss

Sir Francis Carruthers Gould

The last two decades of the nineteenth century produced rapid and striking developments in the newspaper industry which augured well for the cartoonists. The introduction of the halftone block, linotype, rotary press and other technological advances in the 1880s made the large-scale publication of newspapers an economic proposition. What was more, a new and staggeringly large generation of (officially) literate men and women was emerging after the 1870 Education Act and the spread of universal primary education. In 1890 the first fully-illustrated English newspaper, the *Daily Graphic*, came out and was followed six years later by the first unashamedly popular newspaper, Alfred Harmsworth's *Daily Mail* selling at a halfpenny.

The news-illustrators, who had flourished in such publications as *Illustrated London News*, were doomed—their function as observers and recorders quickly appropriated by the photographers. But for the cartoonists it was a new lease of life. Instead of being just weekly commentators, they now had the opportunity of daily editorial statements. The first staff cartoonist had already been employed by the *Pall Mall Budget* in 1888— Francis Carruthers Gould (1844–1925). By the outbreak of the First World War, many Fleet Street papers had established the practice of the daily cartoon. Two of the best known were Poy, Percy Fearon (1874–1949) of the *Evening News* and Will Dyson (1883–1936) whose cartoons occupied the whole of the front page of the *Daily Herald* from 1913.

A distinguished addition to the *Punch* team of this period was Harry Furniss (1854–1925), whose sprightly parliamentary observations recaptured some of the incisiveness of the early nineteenth century, particularly his comments on Gladstone's last ministry which laboured under its cross of Home Rule. The saga of Britain's imperial progress in the '90s was well and wittily documented by Carruthers Gould, no great artist by his own admission but possessing an aptitude for likenesses, in his *Westminster Gazette* drawings. But the most original talent to be discovered early in the twentieth century was that of Will Dyson, whose politically committed attacks won him the kind of unpopularity that cartoonists had ceased to court since the days of Gillray and Cruikshank. His best work—on labour struggles, warmongers, and industrial poverty—was done before and during the First World War. In the twenties he gave up cartooning because of personal problems and when his long-awaited comeback was announced in 1932 it was clear he had lost much of his bite.

1888–1892

FORGERY AND NEW FRONTIERS

The one black stain on the record of peace and prosperity of Salisbury's second ministry was Ireland. The election of 1886 had been a triumph for Unionism and, armed with this mandate and a Conservative Crimes Act Mr Balfour headed for Ireland to do battle with the peasants and their agrarian Plan of Campaign. Parnell himself had moderated his terrorist tactics but the publication in *The Times* in 1888, of letters purporting to be from him approving of the Phoenix Park murders invalidated all his efforts. The discovery a year later that they had been forgeries might have swung the balance back again towards Home Rule, but Parnell—by now involved in a divorce suit—refused to relinquish his leadership and split the Irish party from top to bottom. In Africa however, which the pioneers were rapidly opening up for development and settlement, the story was much happier. In contrast to their record in other continents, Britain, France and Germany contrived to divide up the African territories among themselves peacefully.

1
The Coercion Vulture, Carruthers Gould (1888) There was considerable disquiet in Parliament about Balfour's strong-arm tactics in Ireland. One of the clauses in the Coercion Act denied Irishmen, arrested for violence, the right to be tried by jury. Instead they were sent before magistrates (who were, of course, supported by Westminster). Under his régime, not a few Irish MPs spent much of their time in prison.

2
Penance! Tenniel (1889) Letters purporting to be from Parnell condoning the Phoenix Park murders, and published in *The Times* in a series entitled 'Parnellism and Crime', were revealed at a special commission (set up after Parnell had sued the paper) to be the work of an impoverished journalist named Pigott. *The Times* apologized.

3
Cape to Cairo, Sambourne (1892) Rhodes's vision of a Cape to Cairo railway running all the way through British territory never materialized. What he did achieve, however, in 1892, was a telegraphic link between the two cities.

4
Dropping the Pilot, Tenniel (1890) Probably Tenniel's most famous cartoon showing the Kaiser dispensing with the services of his great Chancellor, Bismarck.

Then we have the Coercion Vulture watching his victim :—

PENANCE !

"HIS HONOUR ROOTED IN DISHONOUR STOOD,
AND FAITH UNFAITHFUL MADE HIM FALSELY TRUE."—TENNYSON.

3

DROPPING THE PILOT.

₊ The Prussian Bully has no further use for Prince Bismarck.

1893–1895

MR GLADSTONE'S PARTY

The Liberal party had entered the lists in 1892 apparently agreed on a new round of reforms (the Newcastle Programme, advocating Irish Home Rule, disestablishment of the Welsh Church, reform of the Lords, triennial parliaments, the end of plural franchise and local controls on the sale of liquor). But Gladstone's fourth and last ministry took office with a majority only big enough to vote his second Home Rule Bill through the Commons, but not to threaten it through the Lords. For Gladstone it was the end of his twenty-five year struggle for peace in Ireland; in March 1894 he resigned and handed over to a Liberal Unionist, Lord Rosebery. For the Liberal party, it was the beginning of the end. Tearing itself to pieces over Home Rule, its leaders quarrelling among themselves, it was overwhelmingly defeated in the election of July 1895 and offered little resistance to Lord Salisbury for the remainder of the century.

1
Attacking the front bench, Furniss (1893) Two studies of the Grand Old Man of British politics during his fourth and final ministry. Both were drawn shortly before he retired from public life.

2
Nearing the end, Furniss (1893) Even over the age of eighty Gladstone never lost his determination to push through Irish Home Rule. Defeat of his second Home Rule Bill, he knew, would be for him final. And so it proved. The Bill passed the Commons by thirty-four votes but, as expected, was thrown out in the Lords. Salisbury's succeeding ministry attempted to allay the troubles 'by kindness' and by solving the agrarian problems, and Home Rule went into abeyance until the next century.

3
Gladstone, May (1893), and

4
The Government Platform, Furniss (1895) In 1894 Lord Rosebery (standing on platform) took over the leadership of the Liberal Party. But after the retirement of Gladstone and defeat on Home Rule, sectional interests within the party asserted themselves and after fifteen months of Rosebery's leadership the Government was defeated on a minor issue (1895). The following year Rosebery also gave up the party leadership.

5
The New Broom, Furniss (1895) For the remainder of the century Salisbury and the Conservatives governed without any formidable opposition.

1

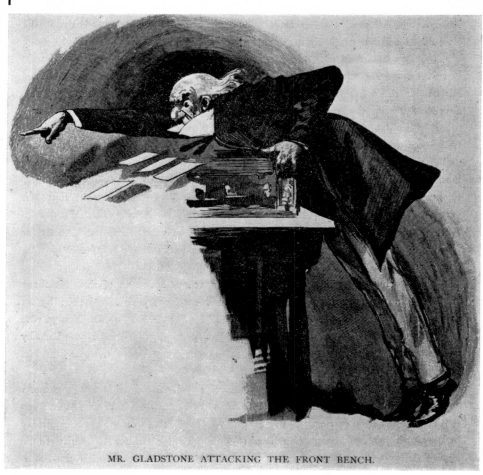

MR. GLADSTONE ATTACKING THE FRONT BENCH.

NEARING THE END: A HOME RULE CABINET COUNCIL.

2

THE GOVERNMENT PLATFORM.

THE NEW BROOM. June, 1895.

1896-1901

IMPERIAL SETBACKS

The promise that the early 1890s had held out of uninterrupted Imperial progress was dispelled by repeated confrontations in the second half of the decade. In the Sudan, where Lord Kitchener was eliminating the Mahdist hordes with the machinegun, a counterclaim by the French (who had reached Fashoda, further south than Khartoum in 1897) had to be met with diplomatic firmness. But a stubborn stand by the United States over a boundary dispute between Venezuela and British Guiana forced Salisbury to submit to arbitration—with not unfavourable results as it transpired—having learnt a salutary lesson from the embarrassing outcome of Britain's bullying approach to the Boers of the Transvaal. The collapse of Rhodes' ill-starred Jameson Raid (in aid of the oppressed Uitlanders against President Kruger) in 1896, strengthened Kruger's position, ruined Rhodes, paved the way for the Boer War and prejudiced Anglo-German relations. In 1899 the Uitlanders formally petitioned the Queen, reciting their grievances against the Boers, and in October war broke out with the British army pitifully inadequate to deal with a campaign dictated by the vastness of the veldt. Only the gallant defences of Mafeking, Kimberley and Ladysmith saved a defeat turning into a disaster, as men died of typhoid by the thousand. Even after victory had been 'officially' proclaimed following Robert's capture of Johannesburg and the flight of Kruger in the summer of 1900, guerrilla resistance by the Boer farmers was kept up for another two years. Nevertheless this did not prevent an imperialist fervour sweeping the Conservatives back into power in the Khaki election in October 1900, and adding 'King of the British Dominions beyond the Seas' to Edward VII's other titles when Victoria's happy and glorious reign came to an end in January 1901.

1
The Greatest Show on Earth, Carruthers Gould (1896) Joseph Chamberlain chose for himself the office of Colonial Secretary in Salisbury's second ministry, and immediately embarked on a policy of conspicuous Imperialism, with the aim of appropriating yet further unclaimed tracts of the Earth's surface.

2
The Jameson Raid, Carruthers Gould (1896) The farcical outcome of Starr Jameson's raid into the Transvaal brought about Rhodes' resignation as Prime Minister of Cape Colony when it was discovered he was implicated.

No. 1. JAMESON, with others, raideth across the borders of the Transvaal. He encountereth the Boers, is overcome, and surrendereth.

No. 2. KRUGER casteth his captives into gaol. Joseph is perplexed. Rhodes cometh to Joseph, but departeth quickly.

No. 3. KRUGER releaseth the captives, who are carried by ship to England. They are haled before the Magistrate, who committeth them for trial. They are tried by three Judges, and are condemned to imprisonment for a time.

"IN A DIFFICULT POSITION."

MAJOR MARCHAND: *Do hurry up with those negotiations—it's very uncomfortable up here.*

3
Fashoda, Carruthers Gould (1898) In June 1896 an expedition under Major Marchand set out to claim the Sudan for France by reaching Fashoda, far up the Nile, which it did thirteen months later. Britain's protests at this backdoor diplomacy—she had been slowly reconquering the Sudan for two years—were so adamant that France evacuated the country within a year. But feeling ran high after the incident for some time (not helped by the outspoken sympathies of the British public for the injustices perpetrated on Dreyfus).

4
A sort of remount system, Carruthers Gould (1902) The guerrilla campaigns waged by the Boer farmers (out of uniform) after the end of the war covered vast areas and kept whole armies occupied for two years. Catching the guerrillas was made no easier by the inferior quality of the horses provided for the cavalry.

1902–1904

NEW ALLIES, OLD EMPIRE

With the new century dawned an awareness of the dangers of isolation and, later, of the growth of the German Empire. Under Balfour (taking over from his uncle in July 1902) the search for new friends went on. First there was Japan, expecting at any time war with Russia but a useful naval ally. Then, in 1904, it was discovered that Britain's long-standing differences with France over Morocco and Egypt were not irreconcilable, and the Entente Cordiale was forged. Against the background of these satisfying diplomatic coups, it was embarrassing, therefore, for the Government to have its Colonial Secretary, Joseph Chamberlain, preaching a policy of Imperial Preference as the answer to industrial stagnation. Neither the Conservatives, the country nor the Colonies were ready for this kind of tariff reform and he was required to resign. But the continuing debate did much to weaken a Government which had already incurred nonconformist wrath (and rallied it back to the Liberals) with its Education Act of 1902, and temperance indignation with its Licensing Act in 1904.

1

An Eastern Entanglement, Carruthers Gould (1902) Britain's treaty with Japan in January 1902 guaranteed the non-intervention of France if war broke out between Russia and Japan (which it did in 1904), and that Britain would have a naval ally if war broke out between Russia and Britain (which it nearly did in 1904).

2

The Great Race, Hebblethwaite (1903) Joseph Chamberlain's resignation from the Cabinet in September to test feeling on his policy of Imperial Preference also brought out leading free-traders. Balfour, steering a middle path between them, continued to hold the party together.

3

The Unemployable, Sambourne (1903) Although in many ways a reformer at heart, Balfour's insensitivity to working-class aspirations led him to ignore large areas of pressing reform. 'Venezuela' on workman Balfour's hod refers to the blockade of that country by Britain, Germany and Italy in protest at its refusal to meet claims for injuries caused during revolution.

4

A tandem team that takes a lot of driving, Heselden (1904) Open squabbling within the Liberals over foreign policy and home rule led Balfour the next year to resign without dissolving Parliament, in the belief that Campbell-Bannerman would find it too difficult to form a ministry.

1

XXXVIII.—AN EASTERN ENTANGLEMENT

Mr. Bull (A.B.): Wei-hai-Wei! Don't you be jealous, I ain't going back there again. I'm going to stick to *you* now. Why shouldn't I have a sweetheart in every port? Blow the consequences

Russia: I wonder what he's up to now!

THE GREAT RACE.

Balfy (To J. B.): Speaking from experience—er, you must have seen my name in the papers—I don't think our opponents will stand an earthly.

2

3

THE UNEMPLOYABLE.

LABOURER BALFOUR (aside). "OUT OF WORK? WANT EMPLOYMENT, DO THEY? WHY, IF I CHUCKED MY JOB TO-MORROW NONE OF *THEM* COULD TAKE IT ON."

A TANDEM TEAM THAT TAKES A LOT OF DRIVING.

"Lots 3 and 4, Piebald Bannerman and Skewbald Devonshire, can be driven together." (Can they?)

[With apologies to Mr. L. Thackeray Edwards (if he will accept them.)]

5
The Race of Death, Sambourne (1903)
A speed limit of 20 miles an hour for
motor-cars was introduced in 1903.
6
In the grip of the American Gambler,
Heselden (1904) The large-scale
closure of mills in Lancashire was
popularly assumed to be caused by the
increase in the US of the price of cotton
by unscrupulous speculators. It was
due as much, however, to the progress
made in America with ring-spinning
while Lancashire industry persisted
with old-fashioned mule-spinning.
7
B-r-r-r-r-r-r-r! Heselden (1904)
Three years earlier Marconi had been
able to transmit messages by telegraphy
across the Atlantic, but Britain's em-
bryonic telephone system was the
cause of much frustration. It was to be,
however, another eight years before
the Post Office was to take over
responsibility for it.

210

5

THE RACE OF DEATH!

IN THE GRIP OF THE AMERICAN GAMBLER.

In order that they may make money, unscrupulous speculators in the United States have raised the price of cotton, and this has closed mills in Lancashire and inflicted untold suffering upon the people.

JOHN BULL: Hullo! Are you there?
NATIONAL TELEPHONE COMPANY: Yes! I am always here.
JOHN BULL: Well, ring off. I don't want you any longer.

1905–1907

LORDS AND LABOUR

The Liberal landslide in the January 1906 election was the most crushing Conservative defeat since the old Tories were discarded in 1833, and ushered in ten years of uninterrupted Liberal rule. One novel feature of the newly-elected Parliament was the presence of a third Party—Labour (twenty-nine seats plus an assortment of Lib-Labs)—and a swift token of its political passion was the passing of the Trade Disputes Act in December, reversing the abominated Taff Vale judgment of 1901 and providing legal safeguards for unions and peaceful picketing. Not even the Lords opposed it, though they were prepared to meddle dangerously with Bills modifying Conservative legislation on Education and Licensing (as they were to meddle with other matters later, to their cost). Britain found another friend, unexpectedly, in Russia but in spite of the European Peace Conference (June 1907) and Edward VII's peregrinations around Paris, Rome, Marienbad and Cronberg the arms race was unabated.

1

The Conference Cure, Raven Hill (1907) In June a Peace Conference, at Roosevelt's suggestion, was held at The Hague. It failed in its attempt to stop the arms build-up and showed quite clearly the direction in which Europe was heading.

2

I believe it's a white elephant, Hebblethwaite (1907) One of the most sensational political victories for Socialism was the victory in the 1907 Colne Valley by-election of Victor Grayson, standing as a Socialist (without Labour Party support) in a three-cornered contest for a former Liberal seat.

THE CONFERENCE CURE.
Scene—*The Nether-Nether Land.*
The Invalid. " WHERE NEXT, DAVID?"

Small Voice: "Good gracious; I believe it's a White Elephant!"

1908–1910

KAISER AND LORDS

To Mr Asquith, taking over from the ailing Campbell-Bannerman in 1908, it must have been difficult to decide which was his most intractable opponent—the Germans or the House of Lords. In October the Kaiser gave an interview to the *Daily Telegraph* saying that the German people were hostile to Britain (and caused a furore in his own Reichstag). The next year the Lords threw out Lloyd George's budget, objecting to the new super-tax and a particularly odious land-tax. The Liberals were determined not to be baulked by the second Chamber and appealed to the country twice in the same year (1910) on the specific issues of Lloyd George's budget and the power of the Lords. On both occasions the results were remarkably similar, giving the Liberals and their allies a clear (if diminished) mandate. The budget went through, and so did a Parliament Bill severely curbing the Lords' veto. The Germans remained, though, and their navy grew stronger every year.

1

The Philanthropic Highwayman, Sambourne (1909) Lloyd George's Bill provided Old Age Pensions for everyone over 70. It was partly to pay for these that his controversial budget included so many novel features.

2

An unrehearsed effect, (1908) When the Kaiser granted his maladroit interview with the *Daily Telegraph* in October 1908, relations between Britain and Germany were already tense. Grey's Anglo-Russian alliance of 1907 had made the Germans feel they were being 'encircled', and Germany's increased naval expenditure had convinced Britain of her territorial ambitions. In the interview the Kaiser confirmed that, though he personally was well-disposed to the British, his people weren't. The resulting debate in the Reichstag (on the *Daily Telegraph* interview) did nothing to make relations less embittered.

3

The Altruists, (1909) Among the features of Lloyd George's 1909 budget were a graduated income tax, death duties and a new Land Tax. This last was highly unpopular with the upper class because it amounted to an additional direct tax, and was objected to in the Lords in that the Land Valuation clauses were not proper to a Finance Bill (which traditionally always passed through the Lords unchallenged). The Lords had never thrown out a budget before and the precedent of them doing so on this occasion brought them into headlong collision with Parliament.

THE PHILANTHROPIC HIGHWAYMAN.

Mr. Lloyd-George. *"I'LL MAKE 'EM PITY THE AGED POOR!"*

AN UNREHEARSED EFFECT.

German Kaiser (*as Conjurer*). "AND NOW, GENTLEMEN, FOR THE BENEFIT OF MY ENGLISH FRIENDS IN THE AUDIENCE, I WILL, FROM THIS SIMPLE PAPER, PRODUCE THE DOVE OF PEACE."

"HALLO! WRONG ANIMAL. MY MISTAKE."

4

Our Airy Nothing, Sambourne (1909), and

5

Recruiting (*new style*), Partridge (1909) In 1905 R. S. Haldane became War Secretary in Campbell-Bannerman's cabinet. After the Military Conversations with France in 1906 (which included detailed plans for sending an army into France in the event of war) he undertook a series of essential army reforms. These included the creation of an Expeditionary Force of 100,000, and of a Territorial Force out of the old volunteers. In this he received the enthusiastic, if shrill, support of Alfred Harmsworth's *Daily Mail* (founded in 1896 and by this time established as the first mass-circulation paper).

THE ALTRUISTS.

Rich Man
Middle-class Man } "I DON'T MIND A BIT ABOUT MYSELF; BUT MY HEART BLEEDS FOR THE OTHERS!"
Poor Man

OUR "AIRY NOTHING."

Mr. Haldane (practising military aviation). "SOMEHOW I DON'T SEEM TO BE FLYING AS NICELY AS I SHOULD LIKE. PERHAPS I GOT MY WINGS TOO CHEAP."

RECRUITING (NEW STYLE).

John Bull. "AN ILL WIND—BUT LET'S HOPE IT'S BLOWING ME SOME GOOD."

1911–1913
ILL-TEMPERED TIMES

A time when political tempers appeared to be permanently frayed. As the Parliament Bill to inhibit their powers of veto trundled on well into 1911, the Lords grew more touchy, proposing more and more amendments until a threat from the King to create 300 new peers silenced them. Trade unionists were militant and labour troubles became acute in August 1911 with strikes by dockers, transport workers, railwaymen and miners in the same month. Women were up in arms over the rejection of their Franchise Bill (March 1912) and suffragettes stepped up their guerrilla tactics. Redmond's Irish party was insistent that Home Rule be implemented at once, now that the Lords were tamed (The Home Rule Bill was duly objected to by the Lords in 1912 but became law in 1914, their deferring powers being limited to two years.) Ulster protestants rioted and demonstrated under Sir Edward Carson against Home Rule. Even measures that were self-evidently desirable, such as Welsh Church disestablishment and the Health Insurance Act (1912), seemed to heap odium on the Government or, as often as not, the unfortunate Lloyd George.

1
The Suffragette that knew Jiu-Jitsu, Mills (1911) In November 1911 there were suffragette riots in Whitehall. Militant ladies continued to clash with police as Parliament rejected one women's franchise bill after another.

2
Unqualified Assistance, Partridge (1912) In July 1912 Lloyd George's Health Insurance Bill came into force, viewed at first with great misgivings by the medical profession. But the Act, which set up a contribution scheme to insure the whole working population against sickness, paved the way for the present National Health Service.

3
The Woes of Unity House, Dyson (1913) 1911–13 were years marked by a series of devastating strikes and great growth within the trade union movement; by the outbreak of war there were over 4,000,000 members. By the Trade Union Act of 1913 the unions recovered the right to make contributions for political purposes, and there was a tendency towards amalgamation—the NUR being formed out of three other unions, for instance.

4
Forcibly fed, Dyson (1912) The forcible feeding of suffragettes on hunger strike in prison had been vehemently protested against by George Lansbury in the Commons in June.

1

THE SUFFRAGETTE THAT KNEW JIU-JITSU.
THE ARREST.

UNQUALIFIED ASSISTANCE.

PATENT MEDICINE *(to the Author of the Insurance Bill).* "NEVER MIND, DEAR FELLOW, I'LL STAND BY YOU—TO THE DEATH!"

2

THE WOES OF UNITY HOUSE.

5

Armaments—their use, Dyson (1913)
The Spirit of Armaments to Peaceful
Peasants: 'What, you go short of food
that I may wax fat! What of it, com-
plaining hinds? What would safeguard
even that meagre food supply were I
not here to prevent each of you tearing
it wolf-like from the other's jaws?'

6

Austria and Servia have a quarrel,
Dyson (1913) Serbia's efforts to gain
independence from the Austrian-
Hungarian Empire were met with
intractable obstinacy from their over-
lords. When in 1914 the Archduke
Ferdinand was assassinated by a
Serbian nationalist in Sarajevo, the
Austrians presented Serbia with an
ultimatum whose terms were almost
impossible to meet. The resulting invasion was to involve all the major
powers in a European War.

7

Not so easy as it was, Dyson (1914)
In 1913 the miners, railwaymen and
transport workers joined forces to form
the Triple Alliance, which was to be the
backbone of the General Strike in 1926.

6

NOT SO EASY AS IT WAS

THE BOSS : " Phew ! The fellers who tied these sticks together knew something ! "

219

1914–1918

TEMPER OF WAR

The quarrel between Austria and Serbia in the Balkans did not concern Britain (even as much as it concerned Germany or Russia). Right up until the invasion of Belgium opinion in Britain was divided on the desirability, or necessity, of getting involved in Europe's war. But once the die was cast and the Expeditionary Force had made its brave stand at the Marne, the country was united in its war effort and patriotic fervour. And that went for the cartoonists whose art was directed into morale-boosting, recruit-catching and Kaiser-bashing channels. Their archetypes were soon established: the British Tommy combined cheerful cockiness with stolid long-suffering, the Hun an over-decorated pomposity with 'silly ass' hauteur. The spirit of treachery, on which they vented their righteous anger, was epitomized by loafers, shirkers, strikers and conchies. The spirit of inevitable victory was, in the absence of any politician who could inspire such sentiments, that good old stand-by, John Bull—as unflappable and it must be admitted as maddening as ever.

1
Arf a mo' Kaiser, Thomas This famous personification of the Tommy's supposedly *insouciant* attitude to the war was printed on posters and postcards and distributed throughout the trenches.

2
Hawking, the sport of Kings, Dyson (1914) Five years had passed since Blériot had first flown the Channel and it was expected that planes would play an important part in the war. In fact for a long time they were confined to scouting or shooting down other planes—it was not until 1918 that they became strong enough to carry a complement of bombs. . . .

3
Forewarned, Raven Hill (1915) It was Count Zeppelin's airship (which had first taken to the air in 1900) which was used when the Germans first bombarded Britain in 1915.

HAWKING, THE SPORT OF KINGS
["The aeroplane must figure largely in the war."—Daily Press.]

FOREWARNED

Zeppelin (*as "The Fat Boy"*). "'I WANTS TO MAKE YOUR FLESH CREEP.'"
John Bull. "RIGHT-O!"

4

Left guessing, Poy (1915) News-papers were instructed not to publish details of the track of Zeppelin raids, just as other war news (such as the withdrawal at Mons) had been censored.

5

Wilfully stupid, Walker (1915), and

6

The camera cannot lie, Poy (1915) Air raids on Britain, a quite unprecedented intrusion, caused immense public indignation and the blackout to operate throughout the country. Yet only eleven hundred people lost their lives in raids in the course of the whole war.

7

The Shirker, Shaw (1915) Public pressure on any able-bodied man to join up was tremendous. At the start of the war any young man in civilian clothes was quite liable to be handed white feathers by girls in the streets. At the end of 1915 it was claimed that 650,000 shirkers lay hidden, but the following year voluntary recruitment gave way to conscription. Public wrath then switched to the few thousand conscientious objectors who were turned up.

8

For traitors, Partridge (1915)

4

WAR LORD : "Where have you been this time? London, Paris, Warsaw, or Rome?"

COUNT ZEPPELIN : "I don't know. It's not in der papers!"

(The Press has been instructed to publish no details of the track of the Zeppelin Raid.)

WILFULLY STUPID.

CIVILISATION : "Your discriminating faculties seem at fault. Just commit those two examples to memory."

5

KAISER : "And as for 'German Atrocities,' will not the world say they are nothing but the malicious inventions of my perjured enemies ? "

CAMERA : "The answer's in the negative !"

(The camera is accumulating a terrible and unanswerable indictment against the Modern Huns.)

THE SHIRKER.
" Did you not hear me call you before? "

7

FOR TRAITORS.
A WARNING TO PROMOTERS OF STRIKES IN WAR-TIME.

8

9

Friend or foe? Downey (1915) It was the job of Lloyd George to keep the factories free from strikes. War-fervour, regular wage increases and his own energy achieved this—but not always. In July there was a strike of South Wales miners, in December Glasgow shop-stewards refused even to listen to him speak.

10

It's a long, long way to Tipperary, Anon Cartoon postcards became a popular form of propaganda, based for the most part on easily recognized catch-phrases, titles of songs, advertisement slogans or just *bons mots*.

11

Our Amazon Corps, Henderson (1916) In 1916 the Army founded the WAACs, which relieved many soldiers for active service. In 1915 women demonstrators had marched down Whitehall with the slogan 'We demand the right to work'. Lloyd George obliged.

12

America to the Front, Raven Hill (1918) In April 1917 the United States, having received no undertaking from Germany that unrestricted naval warfare would cease, declared war on Germany. The Central Powers were confident that the Allies could be defeated before American resources could be mobilized. They nearly succeeded—US forces arrived at the front just before the British offensive at Ypres, but no American tanks and precious few planes ever arrived.

FRIEND OR FOE?

Britannia (to British Workman): "Surely you, who have never failed me before, are not going to play THEIR game for them?"

10

OUR AMAZON CORPS "STANDING EASY."

AMERICA TO THE FRONT.

[In view of the present needs of the Allies, America has not waited to complete the independent organisation of her Army, but has sent her troops forward to be brigaded with British and French units.]

VIII

PRIME MINISTERS
AND THEIR
PARTIES

1916–1922
David Lloyd George, Earl of Dufor (Coalition)

1922–1923
Andrew Bonar Law (Conservative)

1923–1924
Stanley Baldwin, Earl of Baldwin and Bewdley
(Conservative)

1924
James Ramsey MacDonald (Labour)

1924–1929
Stanley Baldwin (Conservative)

1929–1931
James Ramsey MacDonald (Labour)

1931–1935
James Ramsey MacDonald (Coalition)

1935–1937
Stanley Baldwin (Coalition)

1937–1940
Arthur Neville Chamberlain (Coalition)

1940–1945
Winston Churchill (Conservative)

1945–1951
Clement Attlee (Labour)

1951–1955
Winston Churchill (Conservative)

1955–1957
Anthony Eden, Earl of Avon (Conservative)

1957–1963
Harold Macmillan (Conservative)

POSTSCRIPT

1957–1963
Harold Macmillan (Conservative)

1963–1964
Sir Alec Douglas Home (Conservative)

1964–1969
Harold Wilson (Labour)

1969–
Edward Heath (Conservative)

CHAPTER VIII

I n the twentieth century cartoons returned to their rightful place as a popular art-form. Instead of being a middle-class divertissement and erudite commentaries on parliamentary goings-on, the growth of the newspapers and their insatiable appetite for cartoons gave them daily exposure to millions of readers. And events provided plenty of tinder to fuel the fires of their indignation—the massive strikes of the twenties, the hunger marches and unemployment of the thirties, the rise of Hitler and Nazism, the horrors and idealism of the Spanish Civil War, the helplessness and ineptitude of succeeding governments, blackshirts, black marketeers and blackguards galore.

And yet the indignation rarely burned white-hot, the savagery that had been unleashed on Napoleon by their ancestors found barely an echo in their treatment of Hitler or Mussolini. True, David Low (1891–1963) campaigned ceaselessly against the headlong stampede into rearmament, and Philip Zec so infuriated Churchill in the *Daily Mirror* that he tried to have the newspaper closed down, and Vicky waged his dedicated war on Supermac, Harold Macmillan, with something of the single-mindedness of earlier

Strube   *Vicky*   *Low*

generations. But Low's cartoons, brilliant though they very often were, were nearer to sermons than satire, Churchill's fury with Zec was based on a misunderstanding, Vicky's campaign—far from destroying Macmillan—served to enhance the man's reputation.

So what went wrong? What happened was that the very exposure which was such a blessing to the cartoonists at the same time blunted their edge. Editors wanted their readers to be amused (as they still do). Humour rather than wit was what they required, explicitness rather than innuendo, pleasure more than passion. Cartooning by committee took the place of personal vision and, though some cartoonists like Low managed to circumvent it, the editorial policy of the newspaper was invariably the guideline for the staff cartoonist, and the image (often fanciful) which editors nursed of the readership.

Cartoonists developed their own ways of getting through to these vast audiences. Where the eighteenth century had adapted John Bull, British Lions and other universal symbols to their own ends, and where the nineteenth century had accommodated themselves to inherited stereotypes, the artists of the twentieth century invented their own.

Low's Colonel Blimp was his compendium of all the forces of reaction arrayed against peace and progress, just as his later creation, the TUC carthorse, summed up the ponderous advance of the trade unions after the war. Strube's fatalistic little man, popping up in a hundred different guises, often epitomized the frustrations of the ordinary man in the face of irresistible and largely incomprehensible political forces. Lancaster's Maudie Littlehampton was (and continues to be) a kindly composite of certain upper-middle-class pretensions. Giles's motley and octopus-like family identifies the suburban mentality and its ephemeral reactions to events. Many other symbolic characters became household names —such as Poy's double-talking act Dilly and Dally, Cummings's personification of the scourge of the fifties, Mr Rising Price (as well as the ones that are outside the scope of this book like Reg Smythe's Andy Capp and Frank Dickens's office-dweller, Bristow).

The cartoonists of this era could claim, with every justification, to have given a great deal of pleasure but rarely to have affected anyone. The truth of it is that even the politicians ask to buy the originals and build galleries to house them.

1919–1920

MEANWHILE IN IRELAND

The problems of economic retrenchment were not made any easier by the sudden flood of four million demobilized, the rising of prices and the sinking of the pound, and threats from miners, railwaymen and transport workers to begin a national strike. Continued rationing, temporary wage increases and commissions of enquiry staved off the imminent crisis. But the problem of Ireland could not be dodged. In January 1919 the Sinn Fein Congress in Dublin had adopted a declaration of independence, and the Government had responded by reinforcing the Royal Ulster Constabulary with veterans of the War (the Black and Tans). The savagery of the ensuing guerrilla war eventually persuaded Parliament that Home Rule was inevitable, but with adequate safeguards for Ulster. In March 1920 Ulster voted to accept the Home Rule Bill and by the end of the year it had been agreed that Northern and Southern Ireland should each have their own Parliament.

1
Cost of Living, Strube (1919) With the new freedom from price controls, inflation soared. Prices rose twice as fast in 1919 as they had done during the worst years of the war, and wages raced after them.

2
The Wrong Shop, Poy (1919) The taxpayer was staggered to see untold millions spent in never-completed shipyards, and no return in the way of ships.

3
The Kindest Cut of All, Partridge (1920) Lloyd George's convoluted solution to the Irish problem was the Government of Ireland Act, by which there were to be two Home Rule Parliaments, reduced representation for both parts at Westminster and a Council of Ireland (to restore Irish unity). Sinn Fein, however, refused to recognize the southern Parliament, and Ulster refused to recognize the Council.

1

THE WRONG SHOP.

JOHN : " I want to see some ships."
DILLY : " Ships ! That must be another department. *This is only Shipyards !* "

2

THE KINDEST CUT OF ALL.

Welsh Wizard. "I NOW PROCEED TO CUT THIS MAP INTO TWO PARTS AND PLACE THEM IN THE HAT. AFTER A SUITABLE INTERVAL THEY WILL BE FOUND TO HAVE COME TOGETHER OF THEIR OWN ACCORD—(ASIDE)—AT LEAST LET'S HOPE SO; I'VE NEVER DONE THIS TRICK BEFORE."

1919–1920

PEACE AND POSTERITY

On the 18th of January 1919 the Peace Conference opened at Versailles under the direction of the Big Four, as they came to be known: Clemenceau, Lloyd George, Woodrow Wilson and Orlando. Lloyd George found himself adopting a middle course between Clemenceau, whose avowed aim was to extract maximum reparations from Germany and assure the future security of France, and Wilson whose liberal Fourteen Points stipulated the self-determination of peoples, the removal of economic barriers and a 'general association of nations'. This last he achieved, and presided at the first meeting of the League of Nations in Paris in February 1920, but failed to persuade his Senate either to accept the Versailles Treaty or the establishment of the League. Lloyd George had little opposition at home, but the deliberations dragged on interminably, wrangling over reparations, redrawing the map of Europe and continually casting concerned glances at the civil war raging in Russia.

1
Peace and Future Cannon Fodder, Dyson (1919) A truly prophetic cartoon: (right to left) Wilson, Clemenceau, Orlando and Lloyd George leave the conference hall and hear the next generation ominously bewailing the breakdown of their 'peace'.

2
The Big Four, Poy (1920) The protracted negotiations evoked much scorn in Britain, as treaty followed after treaty and conference after conference through the spring and summer of 1920.

3
The Angels of Peace, Low (1920) In June the Supreme Allied Council finally agreed on forty-two annual reparation payments for Germany. Less than a year later French troops had occupied the Ruhr on the grounds of Germany's failure to make preliminary payments—fulfilling the prophecy of Low's cartoon.

PEACE AND FUTURE CANNON FODDER

The Tiger: "Curious! I seem to hear a child weeping!"

"The Big Four."

Millerand   Lloyd George   Foch

THE ANGELS OF PEACE

1921–1922
DISILLUSION

In March Germany announced to the world that she was unable to pay her £600 million reparation bill, due immediately. The British response was to slap a 50 per cent duty on German goods, the French to mobilize an army for the occupation of the Ruhr (France had already occupied Dusseldorf). There were threats of occupation from the Supreme Council; Germany's economic fabric was crumbling and the mark falling fast. In August a state of emergency was proclaimed and in December Germany begged for a moratorium. At home a collapse in the coal export market brought wage cuts for miners—and an immediate crisis. A strike was called in April, which was only prevented from becoming a General Strike by the withdrawal of support from the miners by both railwaymen and transport workers (commemorated as Black Friday in the labour movement for a long time). The year closed with heavy industrial unemployment and every appearance of a continued slump.

1
The Watch on the Ruhr, Raven Hill (1921)   Briand, France's new premier, had occupied parts of the Ruhr at the first signs that Germany was not going to meet her reparation payments. The recovery of the European coalfields had severely affected the British mines.

2
The Decline in Marriage, Reynolds (1922)   Little had been done to meet the need for over 600,000 new houses at the end of the war. The rapid increase in young married couples accentuated the problem.

3
The Solidarity of Labour, Raven Hill (1921)   It was the miners' refusal to accept a temporary offer from Lloyd George which alienated them from the support of other unions.

4
The 8.45, Bateman (1921)   This year the railways were returned from Government control back to private ownership, an amalgam of the old 120 companies into four regional concerns. It did not, apparently, improve punctuality.

THE WATCH ON THE RUHR.

M. Briand (*recruiting for the Entente*). "*Voilà, mon brave*, doesn't that tempt you?"

[May 4, 1921.]

THE DECLINE IN MARRIAGE; OR, THE SPOIL-SPORTS.

"THE SOLIDARITY OF LABOUR."

MINER (*to factory hand*). "WELL, MATE, WE'RE BOTH IN THE SAME FIX."
FACTORY HAND. "HO—ARE WE? YOUR DOOR'S OPEN AND YOU'VE GOT THE KEY
OF MINE."

THE 8.45

1922–1924

PARLIAMENTARY MUSICAL CHAIRS

In the space of two years the country went to the polls no less than three times. His economic reconstruction turned sour, Lloyd George resigned in October 1922 (ironically over foreign affairs) and Bonar Law's exclusively Conservative administration, whose call for 'tranquillity and freedom' was rewarded by a thumping majority in the November election, took over. In May 1923 Law's retirement (and Baldwin's tariff platform) precipitated another election in December, giving Ramsey MacDonald his chance to form the first Labour Government in Britain. From the start, however, it was bedevilled by Labour's suspected intrigue with the Communists. The Labour Conference of 1921 had rejected affiliation with the Communists, but the Government, while disapproving of Bolshevik methods, was anxious to resume diplomatic relations with Russia. When a prosecution against the communist paper *Workers' Weekly* was dropped, the Conservatives claimed it was 'for political reasons' and secured a dissolution of Parliament. The Labour Party was overwhelmingly defeated—not least because of the publication of an alleged letter to the British communists from a Bolshevik leader giving instructions for an insurrection (The Zinoviev Letter), four days before the election.

1
The Charmer, Raven Hill (1921) Disillusionment with Lloyd George's promise to returning soldiers of a 'land fit for heroes to live in' set in. In 1922 a contemporary wrote: '. . . that hero has been shelled out of the lair which he thought secure by the coming of unemployment, as once he was shelled out of the dug-out by the enemy's guns'.

2
The Temporary Servant, Heselden (1923) With hundreds of thousands of workers on the dole, the national papers could still spare a thought for discomforts of the middle class, without even a hint of irony.

3
Much ado about next to nothing, Low (1924) The Conservatives exploited every opportunity of pointing out the Bolshevik menace and Labour's flirtation with the Communist Party.

4
Mother's little Sunshine, Low (1924) The saga of German reparations ground on, causing appalling conditions within Germany. By the end of 1923 the mark had dropped to the rate of 10,000 million to the pound. In October 1924 an international loan to Germany had to be arranged.

236

THE CHARMER.

Mr. Lloyd George. " I trust I have not overrated the mollifying power of music."

[October 12, 1921.]

THE TEMPORARY SERVANT AND HER LITTLE WAYS.

Yet housewives often have to rely upon them in days when the " dole " keeps hundreds of women out of domestic service.

Much Ado About Next To Nothing.

MOTHER'S LITTLE SUNSHINE—FATHER'S LITTLE SHADOW

1925–1927

ELEVEN DAYS IN MAY

'Before I could be called up, the strike had ended. The Poshocracy had won, as it always did win, in thoroughly gentlemanly manner', wrote Isherwood of the General Strike. Its duration (May 3–13) was for the upper and middle classes an interlude of jovial inconvenience, with clerks and undergraduates rushing to drive buses and trains to defeat the strikers. For the miners, whose dispute in 1925 over the threat of lower wages and longer hours led to the strike, it was a do-or-die affair. The mineowners were adamant and outside Government influence. The Royal Commission set up to investigate their grievances found no compromise. At midnight on May 3, after a general lock-out in the mines on May 1, all the transport, railway, printing, heavy industrial, gas and electricity workers in the country stopped work. In the belief that reorganizations proposed by the Commission would be effectively adopted, the TUC called off the strike on May 12—in circumstances which proved unfavourable to many of the strikers and totally unacceptable to the miners (who remained on strike till November).

1
The Red Planet (1926) The West watched anxiously as Chiang Kai-shek's nationalist armies advanced in the north against China's war-lords, stirring up anti-foreign feeling (already high after the shooting of Chinese students in Shanghai the previous year) in their wake. With her goods already boycotted and her Free Ports besieged Britain was forced to come to terms—and harsh ones—with the nationalist movement. By January 1 1927 the Nationalist Government was established at Hankow and another star had indeed dawned in the East.

2
Lèse-Majesté, Partridge (1926) During the General Strike, the TUC at this testing time in its history presented a united front—as did the strike-breakers whose preparations to keep essential transport moving proved particularly effective.

THE RED PLANET.

JOHN BULL. "WELL, ARE YOU GOING TO ANSWER THE MESSAGE FROM MARS?"
SIR AUSTEN CHAMBERLAIN. "WE ARE NOT; IT IS IN ECLIPSE. WE ARE WAITING FOR A NEW CELESTIAL BODY OF THE FIRST MAGNITUDE TO SWIM INTO OUR KEN."

238

INFELIX keeps on walking.

LÈSE-MAJESTÉ.

TRADE UNIONISM (*to Unofficial Striker*). "THIS IS NOT AN ORDINARY STRIKE—IT'S RANK REVOLUTION. YOU'RE NOT MERELY DEFYING YOUR EMPLOYERS AND THE PUBLIC— YOU'RE DEFYING *ME!*"

[*Inset:* John Bull keeps himself in training for a repetition of the recent strike.]

1928–1929

CALM AND CAUTION

If the last few years of the decade were not exactly a Golden Age, then they were certainly a lot less gloomy than their predecessors, a truce between the General Strike and the Depression. In 1928 the nations of the World signed the Kellog Pact outlawing war and providing for a pacific settlement of disputes. At home, even if the miseries of the miners were unabated, unemployment fell to its lowest point between 1920 and 1940 and production rose to a record height. From the government, secure in their great majority, there was some useful legislation including an Unemployment Insurance Act and the Local Government Act, which abolished the Poor Law unions. And there was for the first time in British history One Adult, One Vote with the lowering of the voting age for women from 30 to 21. Little wonder Baldwin went to the polls in 1929 with the cautiously optimistic slogan 'Safety First', but all the more surprising when Labour emerged from the first (and only) three-party election with a bare lead over the Conservatives.

1
Come, come ladies, Strube (1928) (left) Lloyd George's Fund (derived it was said from the sale of honours) was 'to promote any political purpose approved by the Rt Hon David Lloyd George'. In 1929 the Liberal Party, when its fortunes were low, was enabled to fight the election with £300,000 from his fund. (Right) Winston Churchill's budgets were criticized for being erratic, for allowing the Road Fund to run into a large surplus and the Unemployment Insurance Fund to sink into debt.

2
Ordered Progress, Low (1929) The victory of management after the General Strike ensured the continuation of inhuman working conditions for miners for a long time to come, the perpetuation of a class struggle throughout mining areas, and the inevitability of nationalization.

3
The Match of Form, Low (1929) Complete women's suffrage was accompanied by many other signs of emancipation: short hair and skirts, the use of facepowder, even smoking in public.

THE MATCH OF FORM.

1930–1932

SLIDE INTO CRISIS

Echoes of the Wall Street crash of 1929 were heard all around Europe almost immediately. By the end of 1930 unemployment in Britain had reached 2½ million, foreign investors were withdrawing money at such a rate it was clear Britain could only be maintained on the gold standard with an external loan of £80 million. The terms of such a loan were anathema to many in the Labour cabinet, but MacDonald battled on at the head of a hastily-formed 'national' Government to save the pound. By September, however, the country had abandoned the gold standard (1931). MacDonald's Coalition was viewed by the Labour party as a betrayal and, indeed, he was entirely dependent on Liberal and Conservative votes—the more so after the October election in which the Conservatives won 472 seats and the official Labour party only forty-six. Thus encouraged Chamberlain pressed hard for Tariff reform, his cause boosted by the decision of the Ottawa Conference (1932) to favour moderate Imperial preference.

1
Styx Ferry Service, Low (1930) Snowden's (Charon) 1930 budget increased income tax and death duties sharply. Inheriting Churchill's erratic budgeting, he fervently believed that a balanced budget was Labour's way through the Depression, even at the risk of alienating his own supporters.

2
Shade of Uncle Tom, Dyson (1932) The troubles of the cotton trade were symptomatic of the nation's dire economic slide. Between the wars the cotton industry fell from third to eleventh in value of net output, lost a third of its labour force, and destroyed six million spindles in the attempt to reduce its productive capacity and provide higher profits for fewer producers.

3
Here y'are, mister, take it, Low (1932) Under Hoover's Moratorium of 1931, British repayments to the US were suspended. When the moratorium ran out in 1932 Britain was unable to resume them.

4
My dear de Valera, Low (1932) On his resumption as Prime Minister of the Free State, de Valera virtually abandoned the Treaty of 1921. (Left to right: Chamberlain, Baldwin, de Valera.)

5
The Cost of Living, Dyson (1932) The economy measures of Snowden's emergency budget in September 1931 had included 10 per cent cuts in all Government departments including the Navy. At Invergordon there was a naval mutiny over these economies.

242

1

THREATENED INCREASE IN THE HIGH COST OF DYING.

WILL DYSON IS BACK!

SHADE OF UNCLE TOM: *"Somehow dose bosses don't seem never to learn nuffin' nohow!"*

2

"Perhaps some way could be found to give America adequate compensation other than by payment in money."
Says HOOVER

HERE Y'ARE, MISTER, TAKE IT.

" MY DEAR DE VALERA , DON'T YOU THINK YOU MAY BE REGARDING US TOO MUCH FROM THE HISTORICAL VIEWPOINT?"

The Cost of Living—

ADMIRALTY PENSIONS

FORM 8
M 2 WIDOW
PENSION
19/6
SIGN AT BACK

SUBMARINE SECTION

(OFFICIAL)
COST OF LIVING
IS TO GO UP
CHAMBERLAIN

—and the Price of Dying

(Copyright in all countries.)

1933-1935

DEATH-THROES OF DISARMAMENT

By 1934 the threat of German militarism and ambition could no longer be ignored, except by those who chose to (and they were many). In January 1933 Hitler became Chancellor, appointed a Nazi cabinet and proceeded to rebuild the military might of Germany. In violation of the Treaty of Versailles he reintroduced conscription, announced the existence of a *Luftwaffe* and (with Britain's consent) reconstructed a fleet. By his belligerence the Disarmament Conference of 1933 was broken up. The League, too, was having its setbacks: Japan quit after being condemned as aggressor against China, Germany followed shortly afterwards, and the League's one show of spirit—applying sanctions against Italy for her invasion of Abyssinia 1935—was half-hearted. In Britain, though, public confidence in the League persisted and was demonstrated by the Peace Ballot in June when $6\frac{1}{2}$ million people (against $2\frac{1}{2}$ million) declared their support for its ideals. But no sooner had Baldwin won an election, in November, on a platform of 'collective security' than it became plain that the League had failed to save Abyssinia.

1

The All-Heilist, Partridge (1934) On the 30th January 1933 Hitler became Chancellor of Germany and in August of the following year a plebiscite approved the vesting of sole executive power in him as Führer.

2

King Kong, Strube (1933) From the moment the Disarmament Conference opened in February 1932 there was deadlock between France and Germany with the former wanting security and the latter demanding equality. The British Government failed to bring the two sides together on any of the proffered compromises, and in October Germany withdrew. The conference dragged on in an emaciated form until April 1934, when everyone left convinced of the necessity to rearm. Meanwhile *King Kong* continued to thrill cinema audiences up and down the country.

3

Shoulder our burdens, Low (1933) In 1932 the traditional method of protecting the pound (raising interest rates) was abandoned, and the bank rate reduced to 2 per cent. Public expenditure was savagely curtailed, affecting local authority projects and unemployment relief. The building of new schools and roads virtually ceased.

1

THE ALL-HEILEST.

SHADE OF BISMARCK. "I ONCE THOUGHT THAT GERMANY'S GREAT DANGER WAS SOCIALISM. I'M NOT SURE THAT THERE ISN'T AN EVEN GREATER ONE NOW."

" AH, YES. AT A TIME LIKE THIS WE MUST SHOULDER OUR BURDENS CHEERFULLY."

4

You know you can trust me, Low (1935) Baldwin won the general election of 1935 by appearing to support the League, but never had any personal faith in it, and never attended the League Assembly.

5

Noted Fisherman's Eve-of-Budget nightmare, Dyson (1935) Chamberlain's budgets of 1934 and 1935 were presented as hopeful signs of the nation's economic recovery. Income tax was reduced, government salaries restored to their former level and unemployment benefit increased. In 1935 he claimed 'we have recovered in this country 80 per cent of our prosperity'. But in the industrial areas nearly the entire male population was still out of work.

4

" YOU KNOW YOU CAN TRUST ME "

Noted Fisherman's Eve-of-Budget nightmare.

(Copyright in all countries.)

1936–1937

PREPARATIONS FOR WAR

While the politicians peered anxiously at Europe there was little they could take credit for at home. The Depression was at its height, the revised Means Test regulations were accumulating bitterness, in Jarrow two thirds of the male population were permanently out of work. In East London Oswald Mosley's blackshirts were on the march, as were the hunger marchers from the North, cheered on by the intellectuals. But attention to these domestic problems was constantly diverted by the ominous turn of events abroad: Germany was obviously mobilizing, France had nationalized her munitions industry and was extending the Maginot Line, Belgium was forced to impose martial law. Spain had entered into a civil war which was to prove one of the most savage the world had ever known. More than ever it was clear that Britain's paper rearmament had to become a reality. In March 1936 as the result of a White Paper, the country's defence budget leapt up by over £50 millions—most of which was immediately earmarked for the Fleet Air Arm. Yet pacifist hopes were not entirely extinguished: the Labour Party, as late as September 1937, declared war was not inevitable, and in November Halifax's visit to Hitler (in an attempt to reach a peaceful solution of the Sudeten problem) marked the beginning of the fateful policy of appeasement.

1
Jarrow Crusade, Strube (1936) In July of 1936 the special area development scheme in Jarrow (where unemployment was the worst in the country) failed. A contemporary described the town as 'an exhibit in urban lifelessness . . . almost every trader has despaired and put up his shutters. It reminded me of some deserted town in the war zone.'

2
Jumped on, were you? Low (1936) With initial support from Lord Rothermere, Sir Oswald Mosley founded his British Union of Fascists in 1932. Violence was a regular feature of its rallies. The activities of BUF members in the East End of London (blackshirts) resulted in many Jews retaliating by joining the Communist Party.

3
Peace to the poor suffering Basques, Low (1937) Of all the horrors in a horrific civil war, the destruction of Guernica in an air-raid (April 1937) moved the conscience of the outside world more than any other.

1

2

Jumped on, were you? Would you like us to make you a nice cup of tea on the Home Secretary?

"YOU'VE GOT TO ADMIT I'M BRINGING PEACE TO THE POOR SUFFERING BASQUES."

4

The Conscience of the Cabinet, Dyson (1936)   In the summer of 1936 Baldwin's stock had reached its lowest ebb. In June there was a vote of no confidence against him (defeated by the strenuous use of Whips) and he was assailed on all manner of issues from the Means Test to his attitude towards the Hoare-Laval Pact.

5

Organ Recital, Easter 1937, Dyson (1937)   Chamberlain's last budget was a departure from conventional peace-time finance. A special tax, the National Defence Contribution, was levied on those profiting from the manufacture of arms. £400 million was also borrowed to finance aircraft production.

4

(Copyright in all countries.)

THE CONSCIENCE OF THE CABINET
" Where do we go to haunt Mr. Baldwin ? "
"Queue up on the right."
[Parliament opened yesterday.]

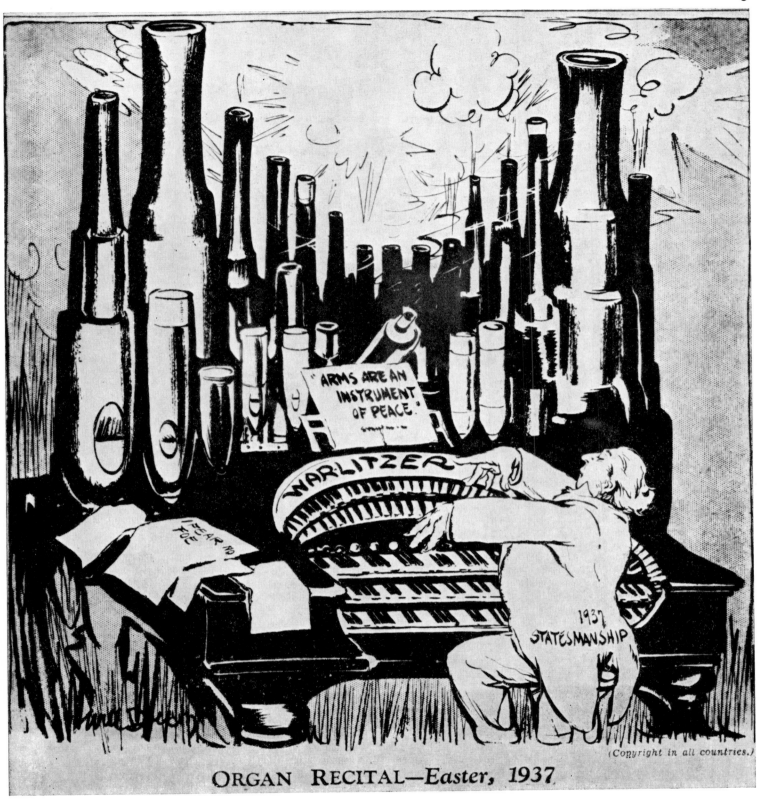

ORGAN RECITAL—Easter, 1937

1937–1939

AFTERMATH OF MUNICH

Chamberlain's policy of appeasing the European dictators started badly, with a row with his Foreign Secretary, Eden, as to whether or not Roosevelt should be brought in. But his visit to Hitler's hideaway at Berchtesgarten in September 1938 blossomed into a top-level Munich Conference a few days later. Sudetenland, it was agreed, was to be transferred to Germany and the remaining frontiers of Czechoslovakia guaranteed. Chamberlain's return from Munich was greeted by Churchill as 'an unmitigated defeat'; by Chamberlain's supporters with adulation. Churchill proved to be nearer the truth. Germany's timetable was hardly held up at all; by March 1939 the dismemberment of Czechoslovakia was complete; in April Hitler denounced the 1935 Anglo-German naval agreement; in May he signed the Pact of Steel with Mussolini (who had already invaded Albania) and in August a non-aggression pact with the USSR. At last the British Government stood firm when Hitler turned his eyes to the north and demanded the cession of Danzig from Poland. On August 25 an Anglo-Polish treaty was signed. On September 1 Hitler invaded Poland. At 11 am Britain's ultimatum to Germany expired; at 5 pm France joined Britain in declaring war.

1

The Autograph Collector, Low (1937) At first, Eden, as Foreign Secretary, was not known as an advocate of strong measures against Germany and Italy—he had acquiesced in the conquest of Abyssinia and deterred the French from action in the Rhineland. He acquired that reputation after his break with Chamberlain.

2

Silencing the critics (1938) Air-raid precautions were the only really positive thing to come out of the Munich negotiations. There had been schemes since 1935, but only on paper. After Munich, ministers envisaged panic in the cities and millions of casualties, and the hasty improvisations of September 1938 only emphasized the real lack of any precautions.

3

A Great Mediator, Partridge (1938) 'Peace with Honour' was Chamberlain's claim after Munich (like Disraeli's before him). His return to Britain was received with relief and rapture.

THE AUTOGRAPH COLLECTOR

SILENCING THE CRITICS

A GREAT MEDIATOR

4

Rendezvous, Low (1939) In August a non-aggression pact between Germany and Russia was agreed. In September Poland was invaded in the west by Germany and in the east by Russia.

5

May West Front, Dyson (1939) Mae West's unromantic approach to life had made her a popular star in the cinema of the thirties.

6

I never touch goldfish, Illingworth (1939) Rumania and Greece had been given unilateral guarantees of military support, shortly after the dismemberment of Czechoslovakia. In July 1940 Rumania placed herself under German protection, but the British evacuation of Greece did not take place until April 1941.

254

" WHAT , ME ? NO , I NEVER _TOUCH_ GOLDFISH ! "

1939–1945
BRITISH AT WAR

The cartoonists approached the Second World War in a different spirit to that in which they approached the First. This time their readers were more intimately involved in the conflict; it was not the remote heroism of Flanders but the chilling reality of nightly air-raids. The readers were also better informed of the progress of the war, through improved news coverage, news bulletins on the BBC and cinema newsreels. The cartoons reflect this, being informed with a deeper awareness of the horrors of war. What humour there was in the war emerged from the personal triumphs of the ordinary man over disaster or inconvenience. Instead of being portrayed as the nincompoops of the First War, the enemy became a formidable opponent—if still a bit pompous. The British Tommy too graduated from the cheeky chappie cocking a snook at the Kaiser to a creditable example of the bulldog breed —and Churchill himself, of course, provided the cartoonists with a ready-made symbol of British tenacity.

1
You may have begun man, Low (1939) A cartoon drawn three weeks after the declaration of war. The struggle was still in its 'phoney' stage and there was a very real danger of national complacency, once the novelty of the new circumstances had worn off.

2
Driver! Wake up! Illingworth (1940) The failure of the army in Scandinavia was responsible for the fall of the Chamberlain Government and its replacement with Churchill's coalition on May 10. When the Germans invaded Denmark and Norway, Chamberlain had claimed Hitler had 'missed the bus'.

3
Is it alright now, Henry? Strube (1940) On August 23 an all-night raid on London marked the beginning of the blitz. Throughout the winter of 1940–41 the capital and large provincial cities were incessantly bombarded, while inhabitants crouched in their Anderson shelters in the garden (and later on in their more substantial Morrison shelters).

1

YOU MAY HAVE BEGUN MAN – BUT I, ADOLF HITLER, WILL FINISH HIM

2

"Is it all right now, Henry?"
"Yes, not even scratched"

4
Tommy, Illingworth

5
I am responsible, Strube (1941) By the autumn of 1941 the German army had advanced deep into Russia and was blockading Stalingrad. Casualties on the Eastern Front were astronomical compared with those in other theatres of war.

6
The bulldog has wings, Illingworth (1942) During the course of 1942, Burmah, Malaya and Singapore fell to the Japanese. British naval power in the Far East was severely shaken, largely because of the vulnerability of battleships to air attack and the meagre presence of the RAF.

7
Poor Fellow, Zec (1942) Public indignation focused not on the shirkers or fainthearted (as in the First World War) but on the racketeers who cashed in on every shortage.

8
The Price of petrol has been increased, Zec (1942) Churchill interpreted this cartoon as an attack on the Government and as detrimental to morale. He sought to have the *Mirror* closed down as a result (through Morrison's intervention it was only 'officially warned' in the end). In fact the cartoon was one of a series against Black Marketeers and was drawing attention to the appalling loss of life in the Merchant Navy from U-boat attacks. In 1942 Britain lost over 3½ million tons of merchant shipping.

9
The Debt Collector, Zec (1943) Indiscriminate area bombing was a feature of Bomber Command's offensive in 1943. The Ruhr, Hamburg and Berlin were the principal targets. On one day alone 7,000 tons of bombs were dropped on Hamburg.

4

"I AM RESPONSIBLE FOR THE PRESENT OF THE GERMAN PEOPLE . . . AND THEIR FUTURE"—HITLER

5

THE BULLDOG HAS WINGS.

Poor fellow... now what can I sell his mother?"

10

Taxi! Giles (1944) In the spring of 1944 raids were concentrated on Berlin. In March US bombers began daylight attacks.

11

Zero hour for the curate, Whitelaw (1944) The Beveridge report, which formed the basis of the postwar welfare state, was first presented in 1942. In 1944 Lord Woolton produced a White Paper on Social Insurance which accepted many, but not all, of Beveridge's ideas.

12

Further retreat is impossible, Whitelaw (1945) In September of 1944 Brussels was liberated, the Americans crossed the German frontier, the Russians invaded Yugoslavia and British airborne forces landed at Arnheim.

13

Here you are, don't lose it again, Zec (1945) On May 1 the German army in Italy laid down their arms; on the 7th Jodl capitulated to Eisenhower and on the 8th (VE Day) von Keitel surrendered to Zhukov near Berlin.

ZERO HOUR FOR THE CURATE

FURTHER RETREAT IS IMPOSSIBLE—Berlin Radio

"Here you are! Don't lose it again!"

1945–1946

LABOUR'S LANDSLIDE

When it was clear that Germany had lost the war, in February 1945 the leaders of the three Great Powers met at Yalta to discuss the surrender and occupation of Germany. When next they met, at Potsdam in July, the line-up was rather different: Stalin was still there but instead of Roosevelt (who had died in April) there was Truman, and Churchill had brought the Labour leader Attlee along, since the country was in the throes of a General Election. It proved to be just as well he did, for Labour gained a landslide victory. It was the first Labour Government with a clearcut Parliamentary majority. Churchill's personal prestige had been outweighed by the store of resentment built up against his party during the prewar years. An immediate economic crisis greeted the new Government with the abrupt ending of lend-lease, forcing it to take emergency fiscal powers for five years.

1
And how are we feeling today? Partridge (1945) 'Doctors' Churchill, Roosevelt and Stalin met at Yalta on February 4, 1945. Among the issues they discussed was the formation of a UN General Assembly.

2
Dumped! Strube (1945) Clement Attlee's win in the July election left him to grapple with some formidable postwar problems, such as the ending of lend-lease, the reorganization of South East Asia, the A Bomb, Palestine and many others.

3
Two Churchills, Low (1945) Churchill resigned on July 26. The electorate applauded him, but voted him out, remembering the miseries of 1930's unemployment.

4
The man who always pays, Strube (1945) In the last two years of the war there had been as many strikes in Britain as during the worst period of the First World War. Despite the limited success of Labour's 'voluntary restraint' wages policy, they continued after the war.

5
The Dead, Illingworth (1946) In September 1946 the Nuremburg Tribunal, giving judgment on Nazi war crimes, sentenced Ribbentrop, Göring and ten other major Nazis to death, and Rudolph Hess to life imprisonment.

1

"AND HOW ARE WE FEELING TO-DAY?"

2

"CHEER UP! THEY WILL FORGET YOU BUT THEY WILL REMEMBER ME ALWAYS"

THE LEADER OF HUMANITY

THE PARTY LEADER

3

THE MAN WHO ALWAYS PAYS

1947–1948
AUSTERITY AND INGRATITUDE

An uncomfortable time in Britain, a period of austerity and shortages. Bread had been rationed since the previous year, potatoes followed in November 1947 (milk, sugar, tea, butter and meat, amongst other products, remained on ration until the early 50s). A particularly severe winter coincided with an acute coal shortage—and ironically with the nationalization of the coal industry. A desperate financial crisis in 1947 (brought about by the attempt to restore the convertability of sterling) was only relieved by severe domestic restrictions and the windfall of Marshal Aid—large-scale financial assistance voted by America for the recovery of Europe. In fact the only people who seemed, and could be seen, to be prospering were the Black Marketeers, 'Spivs' as they came to be known. And abroad Britain's efforts appeared to be met only with ingratitude: her plans for the partition of Palestine were rejected by Jews and Arabs alike; the granting of independence in India was followed by violent Hindu-Moslem conflict; and Russia's attempt to deny the West any access to Berlin in the summer of 1948 was only forestalled by a hastily improvised 'airlift'.

1
The Rope trick, Illingworth (1947) The British Raj disappeared for ever in August 1947. The sub-continent was divided into India, under the government of Pandit Nehru, and the predominantly Muslim Pakistan under Ali Khan. The Punjab, however, continued to be the scene of bitter religious conflict.

2
Competitive selected fruit, Illingworth (1947) Widespread frustration with continued shortages diminished the popularity of Socialist planning—so rapidly that in the autumn of 1947 the Conservatives made sweeping gains in the municipal elections.

3
Fortunate little pig, Giles (1948) The 'Spivs', who could get anything 'at a price' were a familiar feature of the postwar years.

4
Ah Crippso! Strube (1948) A parody of the famous series of Bisto Twins advertisements. The whiff of better things to come was all there was to console the country under the austerity measures of Stafford Cripps (Chancellor of the Exchequer).

THE ROPE TRICK

"You're a very fortunate little pig. When we've done with you, you'll be worth ten times your weight in gold."

BRITAIN CAN MAKE IT
EXHIBITION

AVAILABLE SOON

AVAILABLE LATER

ACKNOWLEDGMENTS TO 'BISTO'

AH! CRIPPSO!

1949–1950
FALL OF LABOUR

The conviction with which the Labour Government had devalued the pound, implemented the nationalization of iron and steel and signed the North Atlantic Treaty in 1949 was considerably muted by their reduced majority in the February 1950 election; further projected nationalization and other contentious legislation had to be put aside. Within months more disasters struck. A dock strike in April was followed by an extension of conscription in September because of the Korean War. The following year Bevan and Wilson resigned (in protest at the imposition of health charges to pay for defence) from a Cabinet already depleted by the illness of Cripps and the death of Bevin. And prices were accelerating at an alarming rate. Himself in bad health, Attlee asked for a dissolution in September 1951, and although the Labour party polled more votes throughout the country, because of their distribution it was Churchill who was returned with a small majority, at the age of 77.

1
Shadows, Cummings (1950) In the 1950 election, the Labour majority overall was reduced to eight, and the ghosts of the Shadow Cabinet (here, Churchill, Eden and Butler) loomed menacingly over every hotly-contested issue.

2
Overcrowding on the railways, Low (1950) The problems of the newly-nationalized British Railways were exacerbated by repeated wage claims. Low's TUC carthorse had become a familiar figure by this time.

3
Pocket Cartoon, Lancaster (1951) Aneurin Bevan's resignation from the Cabinet precipitated a Bevanite revolt within the Labour Party. The Festival Gardens were to be part of the morale-boosting Festival of Britain 1951, but there was considerable anxiety as to whether they would be finished in time.

4
No visible means of support, Illingworth (1951) The Skylon, which has attracted the attention of Messrs Attlee and Morrison, was a striking but otherwise useless feature of the Festival of Britain's South Bank Exhibition.

5
Burning the family ration books, Giles (1951) The return of Conservative Government did not bring an immediate end to rationing: sugar and tea remained until 1952, butter, fats, bacon and meat until 1954.

6
Mr Rising Price, Cummings (1951) became a symbol of inflation throughout the fifties.

266

1

OVERCROWDING ON THE RAILWAYS

2

POCKET CARTOON
by OSBERT LANCASTER

"After all, there is a limit to one's capacity for suffering, and what with all the anxiety about the Festival Gardens and the future of Mr. Bevan, I feel I just can't start worrying about Aly and Rita all over again!"

3

NO VISIBLE MEANS OF SUPPORT

"What do you mean—symbolic?"

(The Vertical Feature for the South Bank Exhibition is now under construction.)

"But, Vera, surely we're being a little premature burning the family ration books."

Mr Rising Price

1952–1953

DAWN OF A NEW ERA

With the accession in February 1952 of Queen Elizabeth II there was much speculation about 'a new Elizabethan Age'. But the Conservatives, while displaying a more united front than the warring factions of the Labour Party, had inherited the same problems, and Butler's approach to the balance-of-payments problem could not differ much from Gaitskell's ('Butskellism', it was soon tagged). They did, however, proceed with some relish to dismantle part of Labour's nationalized empire, notably iron and steel and road haulage. In October 1952 Britain joined the Atomic Club after successful atomic bomb tests in Australia, and the first London Conference of Commonwealth Prime Ministers highlighted the great political strides these countries had made since the war (even if Kenya was being torn apart at the time by terrorism).

1
Smog, Illingworth (1953) Public Enemy Number One was the smog (a particularly dense and lethal mixture of fog and industrial smoke) which settled on London in December 1952. The Beaver Committee was sent to report on air pollution in 1953.

2
Back to base camp, Illingworth (1953) On the 2nd of June the streets of London were packed from dawn with people waiting to see the Coronation procession. Four days earlier Hillary and Tenzing became the first men in the world to conquer Everest—a feat that was taken as good auspices for the new 'Elizabethan Age'.

3
Gently, gently . . . Giles (1953) After repeated discussions, proposals and counter-proposals for a truce in Korea, an armistice was finally signed at Panmunjom in July 1953.

"GENTLY, GENTLY . . ."

1954–1955

THE COLD WAR

With the almost simultaneous invention of the H-Bomb by both America and Russia, the 'cold war' had reached alarming proportions by the beginning of 1954. A Four-Power conference of foreign ministers in January signally failed to reduce world tension. In the US, the Senate struggled to discredit McCarthyism and the President found it necessary to broadcast to the nation on Communism and the H-Bomb. In Indochina the communists took Dien Bien Phu after a heroic siege, and captured Hanoi. Russia threatened to denounce its treaties with Britain if she ratified the Treaty for European Union, and subsequently did so. Yet another Four-Power conference, in Geneva, fell apart on the question of German re-unification (1955). Nor was the Communist menace the only headache Mr Eden inherited on Churchill's resignation in April 1955. In Egypt Colonel Nasser demanded the evacuation of all British troops from the Canal Zone; in Cyprus civil war between the Greek and Turkish communities was imminent; and South Africa's new policy of Apartheid was causing much trouble in the UN and not a little embarrassment to Britain in Africa.

1

Whatsoever a man soweth, Vicky (1954) Verwoerd's Apartheid policy in South Africa, now five years old, had begun to have repercussions among the newly-emergent African states and at the UN. UNO's decision to continue consideration of the 1952 Cruz report on Apartheid led to the withdrawal of South Africa from the General Assembly in 1955.

2

Teddy Boys, Giles (1954) Edwardian-type fashions (long sideburns, long jackets, bootlace ties, tapered trousers and 'winklepicker' shoes) made a sudden appearance in Britain, and the exponents of this fashion were dubbed Teddy Boys.

3

Look here, Sanders, Giles (1955) The exigencies of the Cold War and the published facts about the defection of diplomats Burgess and Maclean, in 1951, had made the Foreign Office especially sensitive on the subject of security. Matters were not helped by the disappearance of the frogman Commander Crabbe during a goodwill visit of the USSR navy to Portsmouth.

4

Of course I know what I'm doing, Vicky (1954) The US hydrogen bomb tests at Bikini in March had revealed to the world the terrifying capacity of the bomb for destruction. The USSR had already exploded a similar device in August 1953.

Whatsoever a man soweth

'Telling me you'd like to give me a damn good 'air-cut, then tan the 'ide off me 'ardly comes under the 'eading of psychological training—do it, Cop?'

"Look here, Sanders—are you watching me or am I watching you?"

"Of course I know what I'm doing."

1956

1

Messrs B & K, Illingworth (1956)
The Russians began the year all smiles,
offering friendship pacts to the United
States and sending Mr Malenkov over
to Britain to inspect electrical installa-
tions. Even Bulganin and Kruschev
came over on a goodwill tour. But the
Cold War was not over, nor had Russian political methods changed. In June
labour riots in Poland were put down
with familiar efficiency and in November Hungary's brave, and unaided, revolt crumbled before the Russian tanks.
Nor could all the UN votes of censure
alter the outcome one iota.

2

Salome, Illingworth (1956) Elected
President of Egypt in June, Colonel
Nasser made it abundantly clear that
he meant what he said about not extending the Suez Canal Company's
concession. In July he seized the
Canal in pique at the US/British opting
out of the Aswan Dam project.
Everyone had proposals at the UN
about what Britain should do about it,
and Mr Eden had his: he bombed
Egyptian airfields while Israeli troops
invaded Sinai. The worst casualty
however was Mr Eden himself who
barely survived the public outcry in
Britain and took himself off to Jamaica
to recuperate. Colonel Nasser held on
to the Canal, even though it was full of
sunken shipping and no use to anyone.

1957–1959

Anthony Eden's inevitable resignation came in January 1957; Harold Macmillan's equally inevitable promotion was announced the next day. To cartoonists he proved a godsend with his air of effortless superiority (he soon became 'unflappable Mac' and 'Supermac') and his penchant for pithy political slogans ('You've never had it so good' he informed a quiescent electorate). Armed with a ticket to the thermonuclear club (May 1957) he pursued his role in international politics with enthusiasm. He flew to Bermuda to reforge Britain's special relationship with the United States. He donned a fur hat to visit Moscow to persuade the Russians that missile bases in Britain meant no harm. He dropped in on De Gaulle, Adenauer and Eisenhower all in the same month (March 1959). In the General Election of October 1959 he was rewarded with an overall majority of 100 and immediately set off for Africa, where he had detected 'a wind of change'.

THE EYE OF THE BEHOLDER

POSTSCRIPT

1960–1970

'Low lived in an age of illusion' wrote Abu, the political cartoonist of *The Guardian*, in 1969. 'Ours is an age of disillusion. Low was lucky. At least he had proper targets to attack: reactionaries, fascists, imperialists, war-mongers. And he also had a degree of editorial freedom which nowadays only the advertisement manager has. Today we have no fascists, but only right-wing democratic parties; no reactionaries, only reaction; no imperialists, only empires; no war-mongers, only wars. Pity the modern cartoonist!' Speaking as a political cartoonist he was surely right of the Swinging Sixties, an arid political decade in Britain, in terms of the stuff that cartoons are made of. There was much far-reaching social legislation, endless freezes, squeezes and wage restraints, incomes policies and balance of payment problems. Occasionally a Profumo scandal or an election came along to whet their appetites, but cartoonists found they had to choose between the trivialities of Permissive Britain with its mini-skirts, pot, pills et al—or if they wanted to make more serious statements to look to the trials of other countries, to Czechoslovakia, Vietnam, America, Biafra. The Swinging Sixties had given the visual arts in Britain a profitable boost but, with a few notable exceptions, the exciting experiments in design, photography and painting passed the cartoonists by, unless it was to comment in a detached way on the excesses of trendiness and fashion. Illustrators, on the other hand, seized eagerly on the new formulae, on the new licence granted them and the new sophistication of readers. In some cases, especially in the underground press and in some glossies, satire, illustration and caricature became indistinguishable.

1
Pocket cartoon, Lancaster (1960) In November D. H. Lawrence's novel *Lady Chatterley's Lover* was ruled not obscene by the British High Court after many years of censorship. This decision was the first milestone in a decade that was to be labelled 'permissive'.

2
European Football Club, Vicky (1961) By the treaty of Rome (March 1957) Belgium, France, West Germany, Italy, Luxembourg and the Netherlands had formed themselves into an economic community to the exclusion of Britain (who had shown a distinct lack of enthusiasm over the project). In October 1961 Britain made a formal application to join and negotiations began in November.

POCKET CARTOON
by OSBERT LANCASTER

"It's an odd thing but now one knows that it's profoundly moral and packed with deep spiritual significance a lot of the old charm seems to have gone."

"HE SAYS HE WANTS TO JOIN — ON HIS OWN TERMS . . ."

3

Berlin, Searle (1961) In August 1961 Britain, Russia and America met at Geneva to discuss nuclear disarmament. The conference was, however, overshadowed by the crisis in Berlin where the Russians had constructed a wall to divide the Eastern from the Western sector.

4

Who's the brains behind this? Jak (1961) In September members of the Campaign for Nuclear Disarmament held a sit-down demonstration in Trafalgar Square and over 1,300 arrests were made by the police. One of the figureheads of the campaign was the philosopher Bertrand Russell.

5

The ability to get to the verge, Vicky (1962) The prolific increase in nuclear deterrents in both Russia and America gave rise to the diplomatic ploy of 'brinkmanship' (seeing how far one could threaten the enemy before having to resort to the use of nuclear weapons). The reality of this dangerous diplomatic game was emphasized by the Cuban Crisis of October 1962. On this occasion Russia backed down (and removed her missile base from Cuba) without plunging the world into nuclear war.

6

Instant Greatness, Birdsall (1963) On the death of Gaitskell in January, Harold Wilson was elected to the leadership of the Labour Party—in spite of having been beaten by George Brown for the number two spot the year before. He immediately became a personality (to the envy of Messrs Heath, McLeod, Maudling and Hogg who were aspiring to the Tory leadership) and his pipe and Gannex raincoat became his indispensable props.

7

But my dear Charles, Cummings (1963) The German Chancellor, Adenauer, declared himself in favour of Britain's entry into the Common Market, but was unable to overrule France's veto.

8

No Entry, Illingworth (1963) In January the British Government heard the result of its application to join the Common Market. It was a categorical refusal—inspired by General de Gaulle's jealous protection of France's leadership with The Six.

3

4

"ALL RIGHT! FOR THE LAST TIME. WHO'S THE BRAINS BEHIND THIS?"

"THE ABILITY TO GET TO THE VERGE WITHOUT GETTING INTO THE WAR IS THE NECESSARY ART" JOHN FOSTER DULLES IN JANUARY

HAVE A LITTLE INSTANT GREATNESS THRUST UPON YOU!

BEFORE   AFTER

"But, my dear Charles, why can't we have a menage à trois—it's a French custom, isn't it?"

UNITED EUROPE PEACE & PROSPERITY

UK 1963

9

The new Church of England, Birdsall (1963)   The publication of the Bishop of Woolwich's controversial book on the 'new christianity' (*Honest to God*) sent shock waves through a Church already trying to get 'with-it' with pop services and a more vigorous and youthful image.

10

. . . that lived in the house that Jack spilt, Steadman (1963)   In June the Government was shaken by the confession of one of its ministers, John Profumo, that he had misled the House about his relationship with Christine Keeler. He resigned the same day. The cartoon also refers to the exposure of Rachmanism in London (the exploitation of slum housing by a landlord named Rachman).

11

Mr Adenauer/Macmillan, Cummings (1963)   Harold Macmillan did, in fact, resign the premiership in October —and out of the scramble for his job the dark horse, Lord Home, emerged victorious.

12

Entry to East Berlin, Giles (1963)   For the first time since the erection of the Berlin Wall in 1961, West Germans were allowed through to visit relatives for a brief period in the Eastern sector.

13

Pocket cartoon, Lancaster (1964)   In May, in accordance with the Pope's ruling on the matter, the Catholic hierarchy in Britain ruled against the use of the contraceptive pill. The decision was widely questioned by Catholics in this country and many continued to use it.

"... that lived in the house that Jack spilt."

11

"You couldn't expect me to resign over the Profumo affair. . . ." And if I go now, it will look like a vote of no confidence in my record of achievement. . . . And Butler hasn't enough support in the party. . . . Hailsham loses his temper, and Maudling's too young. . . . So I suppose I shall have to soldier on, as did . . . . . . that old Chancellor in Bonn."

'One thing I used to like about the Wall—we didn't have to visit Aunt Bertha for Christmas'

12

POCKET CARTOON
by OSBERT LANCASTER

"Sure, Father, an' I thought it was just an aspirin"

14

The Devil we knew, Hewison (1964) In October Nikita Kruschev was replaced as First Secretary of the Soviet Communist Party by Brezhnev and as Prime Minister by Kosygin. It looked to the West as if the 'thaw' which Kruschev's erratic, but comprehensible, personality had made possible was over.

15

The Old Warrior, Giles (1965) On January 24 Winston Churchill died and was accorded the rare honour of a state funeral.

16

Rhodesia, Scarfe (1966) In November 1965 Ian Smith, the Rhodesian Prime Minister, made a unilateral declaration of independence after six months of abortive talks on the 'five principles' on which Britain would grant independence. These included 'unimpeded progress to majority rule' and 'an end to racial discrimination'. Mr Smith's jealous protection of white minority interests, it was believed in Britain, made the attainment of these ends an unacceptably remote prospect.

17

President Johnson and Premier Wilson, Scarfe (1966), and

18

New Boy, Illingworth (1967) Britain's economic position in the mid-sixties became a matter of increasing concern to the Labour Government. In 1966 for the second year running Britain was forced to get deeper into hock with the United States by deferring her loan payments still further. Meanwhile successive budgets heaped all manner of restraints (old and new) on the taxpayer in the attempt to take the country into the black—£50 travel limits, selective employment tax, increased duty on tobacco, beer, wines and spirits, capital gains tax and corporation tax, wage freezes and so on. And so on.

THE DEVIL WE KNEW

"Harry—to treating everybody who came in last night with 'I'm sure the Old Warrior would rather we all had a drink' instead of shedding tears there is a small matter of £5.18.9 outstanding."

15

Gerald Scarfe

"DON'T WORRY, YOU'LL GET USED TO THE SCREAMS..."

19

Start of the Open Season, Heath (1968) The murder of Martin Luther King, the moderate Negro leader, was one of a tragic series of political assassinations (John F. Kennedy, 1963; Malcolm X, 1965; Robert Kennedy, 1968) which stunned America in the sixties.

20

Heart transplant, Heath (1968) Following the temporarily successful heart transplant operations by Dr Christiaan Barnard in South Africa, the world read in their newspapers (and even saw on their televisions) a rush of similar operations—especially in America, Britain and France. There was considerable disquiet over the publicity given to these barely-perfected techniques, and a certain distaste at the public sponsorship given by the British transplant team to the current craze for 'backing Britain'.

21

Paris in the Spring, Lancaster (1968) In May 1968 the students of Nanterre University and the Sorbonne set the tone for a year of world-wide student unrest. Triggered off by the closing of Nanterre, the most violent student riots ever known in Paris raged in the Latin Quarter between steel-helmeted policemen and students manning street barricades. The Sorbonne was occupied and held against repeated assaults for a week. Their example was followed by students in Japan, London, Germany and on several American campuses in the months that followed.

22

Racist! Trog (1968) Many aspects of the Government's Immigration Bill restricting the numbers of immigrants entering Britain stimulated profound heart-searching in Parliament and the Press—but most of all the restrictions on Kenyan Asians holding British passports (whose rights of entry had been enshrined in previous legislation at the time of Kenyan Independence).

23

Well, you said try kicking it, Waite (1969) In July 1969 some 600,000,000 people around the world watched on television as astronauts Armstrong and Aldrin walked for two and a half hours on the surface of the moon. The pictures of the astronauts battling against the low lunar gravity were historic, if not too well defined.

24

So much for the provinces, Trog (1969) In June Prince Charles's Investiture as Prince of Wales was televised to millions of homes from Caernarvon Castle. Stage-managed by the Duke of Norfolk with sets and costumes designed by Lord Snowdon, everyone agreed it was quite a performance.

284

19

The start of the open season.

20

'Things are pretty tense here as the doctor begins to do the transplant operation all over again—only this time blindfold.'

"Ah! Paris in the spring!!"

21

"WELL, YOU SAID TRY KICKING IT."

23

24 'So much for the provinces. When do we open in the West End?'

25
Drawing and Quartering, Waite (1969)
In December 1969 capital punishment in Britain (abolished for an experimental five years in 1965) received its final death sentence. It was argued, however, that opinion polls had shown the majority of the country to be in favour of its retention.

".. BUT SURELY ATTENDANCE FIGURES PROVE THAT THE MAJORITY OF PEOPLE FAVOUR DRAWING AND QUARTERING."

26

It's just as well they believe in the same God, Trog (1969) At the end of the decade, the violence in Ulster which had lain dormant throughout the Sixties exploded once more in Belfast and Londonderry in particular, where entire Catholic areas were barricaded and sealed off from the outside world. With the arrival of 'peace-keeping' British troops, Irish anger embraced them as well, and bomb explosions and sniping increased—till there seemed there would be no end to the continuing Irish problem.

27

The airport is closed, Waite (1970) An epidemic of hijacking hit the world's airlines this year. At the height of summer hardly a week went by without at least one plane being diverted to Cuba or North Africa or Korea. The most daring coup came from Jordanian guerrillas, who succeeded in capturing three planes on the same day—and eventually blowing each one of them up. At Heathrow, however, there were additional reasons why passengers didn't make their destinations: the airport was bedevilled with strikes all through the year.

28

Did we win, mama? Rigby (1970) In January the civil war between Nigeria and its breakaway state Biafra came to an end with the flight of the rebel leader, Colonel Ojukwu, to the Ivory Coast. In the later stages of the war (and after its conclusion, before proper relief flights were organized) it was estimated that over a million Biafrans died of starvation.

29

General election 1970, Willson (1970) During the run-in to the election, public opinion polls showed that the swing to Labour was sufficient to ensure its comfortable return to power. They were uniformly wrong.

27

"Did we win, mama?"

28